Blackbird

The Story of a SistaMom

RAHKAL C. D. SHELTON

First Printing: 2018

Printed in the United States of America

ISBN: 978-0-692-06445-0

Rahkal C. D. Shelton
Atlanta, Georgia 30318

Blackbird

www.rahkalshelton.com

Instagram: rcarladanielle
Twitter: rcarladanielle
Facebook.com/rahkal.shelton
www.youtube.com/c/rahkalshelton

Cover Design: Rahkal C. D. Shelton
Cover Illustration: Lindsay Dabney
Editing: Lisa Thompson writebylisa.com and Kathy Curtis
Typesetting: Kathy Curtis

Most names and some identifying details, passages, and scenarios have been changed to protect the privacy of individuals.

DEDICATION

To my beloved grandparents, Ethel and Robert Dockery: Thank you for everything. I miss you.

Brenda and Lawrence Matthews: I never imagined losing you both so soon. Thank you for everything. Both of your legacies will forever live on until I live no more. I love you.

Raven Tenisha Taylor and Xavier Jabarry Tarver: From the bottom of my heart, thank you for challenging me to be a better woman, guardian, mom, sister, and human. I promise always to protect, love, and care for you. You both are more powerful than you'll ever know. You are fighters, warriors, resilient, confident, talented, smart, creative, amazing, and every other affirmation we've repeated over the last year. I am so proud of you. Thank you for trusting me with your stories. Thank you for allowing me to share a glimpse of what you've overcome. There is power in owning the not-so-pretty things in life. By owning them, they can't own you. It's power in vulnerability. I've said this often and honestly—believe it, I needed you as much as you needed me. Cheers to a beautiful life together. Forever TTS.

TABLE OF CONTENTS

Acknowledgments.. vii

Introduction ix

Chapter One...............Raven = Blackbird..................... 15

Chapter Two................Ms. Independent........................23

Chapter Three.............Guardian Angel..........................29

Chapter Four ....The Call.......................................35

Chapter Five................Man Man 43

Chapter Six..................Terminal C 49

Chapter Seven ....Syrup Sandwiches.....................55

Chapter Eight..............Lights, Camera, Action!..........61

Chapter Nine...............F*ck Cancer 65

Chapter Ten.................Hey, Girl, Hey 71

Chapter Eleven ....Dreaming Bigger.......................75

Chapter Twelve...........Everything Is Fine 79

v

Chapter Thirteen........**Deep Breaths** 85

Chapter Fourteen ......**Two Months Later**....................91

Chapter Fifteen...........**They Can't Take Us**.............. 103

Chapter Sixteen..........**Here Goes Nothing** 117

Chapter Seventeen ....**Blackbirds Fly** 121

About the Author 125

ACKNOWLEDGMENTS

A number of wonderful people have intentionally been placed in my path during this season in my life. Words can't begin to articulate my gratitude for you. To my friends, best friends, family, mentees, and all my loved ones, I value you beyond words. I am grateful for each portion that you've deposited in me. Pee Wee (girl, what would I do without you?), Billy Taylor, Rahkal E., Kim and Joe, Kenya, Indiana, Bakir, Jamie, Stephen, Marilyn, Damaris, Devin, Okenna, Undralyn, Dwayne, Bronchelle, Mr. Freeman, Mr. Featherstone, Raven and Xavier, Larry H., James E., Isaiah B., The Muse & The Messenger, Roberto, Anna, April, Val, Kim, and my 6SW family: I couldn't have done this without your support! Thank you to my editors and all creative/social media/promo personnel. Parenting has my memory all over the place these days. Please don't take it personally if you were not mentioned by name. I love you!

Ma· tri· arch
ˈmātrēˌärk/
noun
A woman who is the head of a family or tribe.
An older woman who is powerful within a family or organization.[1]

---

[1] Definition of matriarch, *Oxford Dictionary*, https://en.oxforddictionaries.com/definition/matriarch. Accessed January 13, 2018.

INTRODUCTION

~~~~~~

Bertha Matthews, 67
Home Health Hospice (Lung Cancer)
Calumet City, Illinois

Dreamed of those blackbirds again. This time, they were flying in a formation over a crowd of people. Only three of them. One was up front, leading the other two.

The lead bird was the strongest one with the most beautiful black wings and reminded me of someone in my family. Can't put my finger on who, but, honey, family is the reason I'm still here today. And God, of course. Just the thought of them makes it hard to swallow and tears well up in my eyes. Despite all the "told you so" and me fussing, still, I know they know I love them. You see, I was diagnosed with Stage III lung cancer nearly two years ago. It's Stage IV now, but I'm still here, at least for a little longer anyway. And you know what? I'm thankful. It's never a use feeling sorry for yourself. You just keep going with what you have.

And this time, I'm trusting my family to keep going when I leave. I'm from the old-school way of things. I was taught you have to protect, honor, and love your family. And blood is thicker than water—don't let nobody tell you different. If you don't have family, what do you have, anyway?

Mama had four of us: me, Billy, Carlos, and Misty. Misty is our autistic sister, the youngest that I been caring for since Mama died nearly thirty years ago when I was in my thirties. It's been a journey since. She taught me everything I knew. I've been cooking full-course meals since I was eleven: baking, cleaning, sewing clothes, doing laundry, and handling family affairs. Mama trusted me young, and as the old folk would say, I always been ahead of my time. I did everything and took pride in being the second in charge under Mama.

My name is Bertha. Bertha Matthews or Auntie Bertha. I'm the matriarch of the family. I've been the glue after Mama left. I cared for my brothers too, especially Carlos. He's my baby brother. Damn near sixty-five years old and still messing with that stuff. Hasn't been able to shake it, been on drugs his whole life. He's made some hellish decisions too because of it. I ain't making excuses for him, but he has, and I've bailed him out each time. Carlos is a street dude and a hustler. He could talk a fish right out of water.

That's what he does and does it well. What angers me most is the kids. He has a couple of them, and I've helped to raise each of them off and on.

That's what family do, right? We step in. These children didn't ask to be here. And Lord knows, I've worked to make sure they weren't taken away or lost in the system. They're the real reason I've run to my brother's aid time and time again.

All his kids are grown now except for two. Surprisingly, he still making babies and has a ten- and an eight-year-old. I met them a couple of years ago and been looking after them until I couldn't do no mo. This cancer has been a battle that I've fought solo. I didn't have the courage to tell anyone other than a close friend or two. Most days, I'm weak or just suffering in pain. It seems like radiation broke my body down further than it was. Been this way a couple of years now. Truthfully, I didn't want anyone worried about me. I didn't want them splitting up my family or taking away my grandbaby because of my illness. I been caring for one of my grandbabies since six months; he's four now. He's the son of my second oldest son.

Me, Billy, and Carlos all have grown kids with kids, and I've helped to raise everyone's kids. Keep the family together, cousins need to know each other is what I used to tell Billy and Carlos. I have four handsome sons myself, and every holiday, birthday, or just because, I hosted my nieces, nephews, and siblings over. Hell, even people from the neighborhood knew they were welcome. I never met a stranger. I cooked up all types of food and baked desserts from scratch. We would have music, games, and fun. I took pride in being there for my family.

My boys are all grown too, but my youngest is my special child. He's my heart, my ironman, and has stayed with me the longest. He's been my caregiver the last few years. Recently married with kids, doing well for himself, and has a career as a firefighter. I'm so proud of that boy. He's also one of the biggest reasons I didn't tell anybody about my cancer. I especially didn't want him stressing out or agitating his heart.

We found out about his heart problem some years back. He's my miracle child. I'm so very proud of that boy. I ain't want him worrying about me, so I fought all the way till the doctors said there was nothing else for me to do. My child knew something was different. I could feel it. My pathetic excuses of being sick weren't adding up to him, and even after he learned I had cancer, his optimism flowed. He promised not to tell anyone but assured me I'd be okay. "You're going to beat this, Mama," he'd say. My boy has always been brave.

He and his first cousin, Carlos's oldest daughter, are very close. They like two peas in a pod. I know she keeps him encouraged, levelheaded, and going. She's my special niece and the one that went off to college. She graduated twice, even got a second degree and making a name for herself.

She's responsible and a lot like me. I admire things in her. As I think of it, that's who was in my dream. She was that blackbird leading the other two. My gawd, that blackbird was my niece, Danielle!

It takes a lot of respect for her to do right by her father. Lord knows, Carlos ain't never been there for any of his kids. Despite them not having a relationship, she still goes to see her ten- and eight-year-old half siblings ever since I told her about them a couple of years ago. She stops by to feed and check on them. She even looks after Carlos at times. She's done that faithfully until she moved down South to chase her dreams. We were sad to see her go, but I'm truly happy for her. I'm proud of all my nieces, nephews, and grandbabies. I am proud of my family.

I think I did some good. I have fond memories of my beloved family. Each of them has a special place in my heart, and I know I've carved one in theirs. I'm trusting God that they will keep the family together and carry this torch that I been burning. With that, I believe I can move on now.

CHAPTER 1

RAVEN = BLACKBIRD

Inglewood
South Side – Chicago, Illinois

"**B**itch! I'ma kick yo mutha-fucking ass! Don't you play with me, bitch!"

Yelling followed by distant screams bounced off the cloudy glass and plastic that covered Raven's tattered window. The couple from 1503 was arguing as they did each morning, just loud enough to wake Raven and her brother, Man Man.

"Get up! Man Man, you ugly black bastard, get up."

"Ohhh, Raven, just lay back down. We probably too late anywayz, and they not gonna make us get up today. It's Friday, and school almost out."

"I know, Man Man, that's why we need to get up. So get up!"

Raven stood about four feet eight inches tall and was sixty-eight pounds soaking wet. Very petite and slender in build, she reached over her brother to grab a dirty red-collared shirt hanging from a shopping cart that took up most of the space in their shared room. It had been the fourth consecutive day she'd worn it.

Jumping up as she pulled it over her oven-roasted, beautiful, dark-brown skin and nappy, untamed head, she yelled again, "Get up, Man Man, now! We have to get to school."

Raven loved school and the opportunities to learn new things. Most importantly, school guaranteed something to eat for the day. Like most kids in her building and neighborhood, school gave them a temporary escape from hunger, drugs, hopelessness, and the possibility of being jumped on or shot.

Although most of the fighting took place outside of school, sometimes it happened at school. Even at the elementary age, gangs and gun toting existed. Raven and Man Man knew this because they had friends who banged and brought guns to school.

It was the cool thing to do, and sometimes it was just needed for protection. At least, that's what Man Man thought. He watched and listened carefully to anything sensational or of street interest.

Man Man, a shade darker than Raven, stood about an inch shorter. He had a distinct gap in his teeth that complemented his smile. Man Man was charismatic, very outgoing, and couldn't sit still. He rocked with anticipation and talked a mile a minute with questions, comments, jokes, or more questions. He had his father's eyes though his weren't nearly as shotty as his cocaine-addicted parent's.

Raven and Man Man lived on the South Side of Chicago in one of the most vicious neighborhoods in Inglewood where gunfire, drugs, gangs, and murders were all too familiar. Truthfully, they were desensitized to the violence and watching fight after fight between their parents didn't help.

Man Man was nearly three years younger than his ten-year-old sister, Raven. He was the more street savvy of the two but still held onto her every word. After all, she was the oldest and turning eleven soon. Her smile and the memorable beauty mark that rested on her left cheek complemented her perfectly. Her eyes were innocent, sassy but curious, and full of hope. She was determined to find a new life for herself and her little brother.

"Move over, Man Man," sighed Raven as she elbowed him in the stomach.

They both stood in the dirty, desolate, and dim restroom with their pointer fingers stuck in their mouths. They rubbed their fingers against their teeth in a back-and-forth motion before filling their hands with drops of tinted water to gargle and spit. The stench of urine filled the air, and roaches crawled about their feet. The walls were stained with filth and the tub with built-up dirt and gunk. There wasn't a need for showers anyway because there was hardly any soap. Furthermore, their parents didn't really bathe or require them to.

"Man Man, Raven move," the frail, black figure shouted as she pushed them both before pulling down her shorts to sit on the toilet.

"Man Man, get out, don't you see my pussy out."

"Ma, I was in here first," Man Man emphasized before storming out.

"Boy, don't you talk back."

"Raven, I'ma meet you outside," Man Man sighed.

Raven looked over at her dark-complected mother, and they locked eyes for a few seconds. Raven felt hurt, frustration, and sadness all rolled up in a bundle of pain. But at ten years old, she didn't know how to express or process the emotions she felt.

"Raven, when y'all get home, come up over east so we can hit this lick. You know the people get paid today. We need some of that money. You hear me, girl?"

"Yes, I hear you. Bye, Ma." Raven stormed out.

She and Man Man met downstairs near the busted fire hydrant in front of their building.

"Ma said that we need to go over east and hit this lick after school. Make sho you meet me when the bell rings," she instructed her little brother. The two walked several blocks, making their way to their elementary school.

The crossing guard out front smiled as she greeted her. "Morning, Raven. How is my little blackbird? I have some knickknacks for you. I'll give them to you end of the day."

"Aww, Ms. Washington, you always calling me blackbird."

"Well, Raven, you draw the most beautiful blackbirds. After all, your name is Raven, and what's that, honey? A blackbird. Have a great day, beautiful. You too, Man Man."

"Hey, Ms. Washington." Man Man waved before entering the building.

Raven was such a beautiful girl with a wealth of talent and potential. She enjoyed gymnastics, sports, dolls, drawing, creating, and caring for people. Extraordinarily nurturing and sweet, she looked nothing like the chaos she was birthed into, internally anyway. Externally, things were different. Her hair typically sat all over her head. Her lips were chapped, but her smile was still engaging. Raven was a true diamond in the rough. She was a dreamer and could easily get lost for hours in her creative side.

Drawing was Raven's top way to escape. It was her coping mechanism to help endure many of the traumatic events life had handed her. If she wasn't watching her parents get high, her father would be very physical to her, Man Man, and their mom.

She and Man Man often hid under the bed to avoid blows from Carlos. Their mother wasn't any better. The verbal abuse toward Raven specifically was degrading at best. But she preferred words any day over punches to her stomach. These were brutal. Coincidentally, after each beating, Raven's drawings progressed.

Her favorite thing to draw was blackbirds. She'd start with the wings, extending them into the body. The wings of her birds were always exaggerated. She believed that the larger the wings, the further they could fly. Deep down, Raven wanted to be just like the birds she drew. They were a symbol of freedom. *Birds have the best lives; they sing, eat, and fly*, she thought.

Unfortunately, she didn't have her own set of wings to escape her home, community, and environment.

"Raven, are you following?" Her teacher snapped her out of her trance. "Put away that sketchbook now, young lady, and go to the board," he demanded.

Nervous at being singled out, she got up from her seat. Although Raven loved learning new things, she lacked confidence and needed a lot of support academically. She and Man Man lacked elementary fundamentals and were both levels and a grade behind.

The previous year, they were absent forty-plus days and tardy for at least as many. No one checked for homework or helped with anything, and they still were reprimanded for failing grades. Their parents' only concern was getting a check to get high.

Students dispersed from every door as the bell rang. Man Man met Raven near the back exit door, the same place they met every day. "Man Man, don't forget we need to meet Ma over east to make some money."

"Yeah, okay, Raven, I got a couple of things to do first. I'll be that way later," Man Man declared.

"Come on, we not suppose to split up," Raven responded.

"Okay, Raven," Man Man walked off in the other direction with a devilish grin on his face.

Flashing her student ID, Raven hopped on the bus going in the direction she needed to meet her mother. "That'll be twenty cents, little lady," the bus driver demanded.

"Sir, I don't have any money and need to meet my mother," she explained before heading to the nearest seat.

"You kids know your ID is for discounted rates. Have your money next time, or you won't be going nowhere," the bus driver huffed.

Looking out the oval window to her left, Raven spotted three blackbirds sitting on the street lights above. She closed her eyes, remembering:

"Raven, this is your big sister; her name is Danielle," Aunt Bertha smiled as she introduced the two sisters.

"Hi, pretty girl, how old are you?" the brown-skinned friendly face uttered. Raven put up three fingers before her Aunt Bertha chimed in.

"She doesn't talk much, but she's three. I keep telling Carlos they need to be in somebody's school."

"Wait, 'they?' Is there another child? How many other children does he have?" Danielle inquired.

"Raven has a brother. I think he's ten months or something. They just started coming around. Well, I started going to get them when I learned they were out there," Aunt Bertha explained.

A voice broke into Raven's thoughts. "Excuse me, young lady, is this seat taken?" the busty woman carrying several grocery bags asked, snapping Raven out of her daydream.

Chapter Two

Ms. Independent

~~~~~~

**CNN Headquarters,
Downtown – Atlanta, Georgia**

*C*heck on your mentees and your sister, make a contact list, and price those business cards, Danielle thought as she mentally began compiling her weekend's to-do list. "It's been a hectic but successful week," she said aloud, crossing her legs before lying back on the plush, red-leather sofa of the sixth-floor break room.

Her lunch break was intentionally spent checking in and catching up with family. Danielle had landed her dream job in Atlanta three years prior after relocating from Chicago. It was hard balancing work, personal, and her entrepreneurial side. She hardly made time for herself, let alone family. So on lunch breaks, she cackled and video chatted, getting lost in conversation with her loved ones.

Danielle, a five-foot three-inch, toffee, brown-skinned young woman, had a smile bright enough to

23

illuminate the state of Texas. Her modesty and heart were even more radiant than her smile. Many viewed her as a mover and shaker, no-nonsense professional by all accounts. Her relentless ambition and perfectionism often became her downfall.

Danielle graduated *cum laude* from Texas Southern University in Houston in 2007 and then received a master's in media communication. As the first in her family to graduate and go off to college, she had a point to prove. After all, her upbringing was the polar opposite of her current life. She wanted to set a new bar and expectation for her family. She wanted to make them proud.

"Girl, you know I'ma need a badass dress for my release party," she told her best friend, smiling at her cell. They had been friends since undergrad and were looking forward to connecting at Danielle's book release party.

Only months away from publishing her first book, Danielle beamed with anticipation but was also very nervous.

"No, ma'am, we will not have you looking hot and thotty at your party. We should think classy but sexy," her friend suggested. "Either way, you'll be badass in whatever dress we get to hug those hips of yours."

"Okay, I have to run and get ready for this meeting. Love you, girl," Danielle blushed.

Danielle hung up quickly, finishing her smoothie before pulling out her compact mirror to touch up her lipstick. She was beautiful and seemingly well put together. However, a darker side lay behind her gorgeous almond eyes. An insurmountable longing lived inside her, but she masked it well, filling her idle time with goals, ambitions, sometimes guys, and new tasks.

Strictly speaking, moving to Atlanta made the most sense for her career. She didn't want to leave her family and friends but knew she needed to make the change. After working on her book for years, she was thrilled to be so close to conquering that goal. Holding her release party in Chicago was a no-brainer. What a way for the prodigal child to return!

Her phone vibrated again before she picked up. She had to take this call. It was one of her favorite people.

"Hey, cuz, what's good?" the deep voice on the other end of her phone said.

"Hey, I really need to run into this 1:15; everybody okay? What's up?"

"Yeah, all good. I understand you busy, Mary Jane Paul. We'll chat later," he chuckled. (Mary Jane Paul was a successful fictional television news anchor devoted to family.)

"K, call you back later." She sighed before adjusting her fitted pencil skirt, taking a deep breath, and walking into the conference room at the end of the hall.

Ending the call was painful for him. He needed to break some not-so-good news to his favorite cousin. But he knew this year was critical to her. After all, he was her biggest cheerleader.

He was born on September 9, 1981, a too-cool-for-school, light-hearted, goofy, and precocious kid.

He hit the scenes dancing to MJ's "Wanna Be Startin' Somethin'." By the time she arrived, they were grooving to "Thriller"—true 80s babies, three years apart, kissing cousins, and partners. They were best friends!

His name, Lewis Matthews Jr., but she called him Larry. He went by a couple of names: "Larry," "Lew," or the self-proclaimed "Big L" when he'd rock his bucket Kangol just like LL Cool J.

Larry was her big cuz but truthfully was more like a brother. He was the cousin who dressed fly and had what they called "360's"—waves in his hair. The ones that got the girl's seasick. Yeah, those.

He had everything—the looks, leather jackets, Timberland boots, gold chain, confidence, and even a driver's license (growing up). There wasn't a thing he couldn't do. He and Danielle talked for hours about everything. They stayed up late, laughed, and stole his mom's car when they were younger just to joy ride.

Larry was fearless, confident, and just so chill. Just like his mom, he never met a stranger, never complained, and hardly ever uttered a negative word.

Danielle's cousin was very optimistic. Even the times they got caught or got in trouble, he took responsibility. He was accountable and easily let things roll off him.

Larry was one of her biggest fans when she went away for college. They didn't envy each other, have spats, or do the drama thing. He was just too cool for any of that. That same coolness got him through one of the most significant challenges that he faced at age twenty-five.

She distinctly remembered his call. "Yeah, cuz, I'm in the hospital for this little thing, but I'll be there for your graduation. Give me a couple of weeks. We 'bout to kick it hard down in Texas."

The whole time, he neglected to tell her that the "little thing" was a developed rare heart disease and that he needed a transplant. She knew he was fearless and optimistic, but after learning he had heart problems, she thought he was crazy. In his mind, that "little thing" was nothing. He thought they would be partying in Texas on graduation night.

Meanwhile, she and the family were caught entirely off guard by it. They didn't understand how it happened.

Larry was in military shape, never drank or smoked, and he never had heart issues. But the way he handled this spoke to his character. He didn't sweat many things, not even after learning he had a failing heart.

Years prior, he and Danielle made a pact with each other. They promised to take care of their families, to become successful together in their 30s, and to always challenge each other.

Diligently working on his end of the bargain, he became a firefighter just two years after a successful heart transplant. They both felt as if God gave him a new heart and a second chance at life. With that, he wanted to save other people's lives. Larry loved everything about being a firefighter.

Danielle watched him grow mentally, physically, and professionally into a fantastic man, father, husband, son, and friend. That transplant changed his life. In their 20s and 30s, they both went on to do some epic things. Their relationship was beyond close.

Despite their close connection, she didn't hear the sadness in his voice or hear his heart breaking as he held the phone to his ear. Busy and on the go as always, she promised to call him back.

This time, though, the news wasn't about him. He'd called to tell her his mom, one of her favorite aunts, had been diagnosed with cancer.

Chapter Three

Guardian Angel

~~~~~~

53rd/Hyde Park
Chicago, Illinois

"Excuse me, excuse me. Y'all got a couple of dollars to spare? My babies is out here hungry. I'm trying to make sure they got something to eat. We need to get them some shoes too," the frail, black figure demanded.

"Nah, ma'am, I got nothing for ya," a passerby shouted.

"Where the fuck is Man Man? I said y'all meet me over east after school. Not just yo black ass. You hear me, bitch? Y'all messing with my money. He smaller than you, and people mo likely to give up them coins." The frail, black figure hurled as she towered over Raven. Spit flew from her crusted, bleeding, cracked lips as she spoke.

"I don't know where he at. I told him you said meet over east, but he walked toward the building anyway, so I hopped on the bus," Raven defended.

"Alright, if this ain't working today, we going to the store, get some Pampers, then flip them."

Raven eyed her mother, holding onto every word but daydreaming of other things. When they went out to make money, she often worried about getting caught. Her mother didn't seem to care. If they weren't on the corner begging for money, they'd hit a local store to steal and sell diapers in the building they lived in.

Raven's mom, Renesha, was a dark shade just like Raven, frail, and looked as plain as sheets of paper. She was an older woman stained with her addiction, cycle of poverty, mistakes, and young children that she couldn't care for.

Surprisingly, she and the kids' father, Carlos, were able to conceive healthy babies, given their ages and years of drug abuse. Heroin and cocaine addicts, they both had other children who were either taken away by Family Services or raised by another family member.

Raven and her brother had a couple of Family Service scares, but the love of their Aunt Bertha kept them together. Carlos couldn't afford to lose the kids anyway. They were a primary source of income. Rather than hustling, stealing, or receiving government assistance, the kids' existence was put to use.

Raven started to feel and notice this. As she got older, her parents begin to resent her badly. They thought she "knew too much" and was getting too smart for her britches. Man Man received a little more compassion as the younger child. He didn't see them like Raven did. And because she began to see them, the visibility of the bruises they inflicted on her became more apparent.

She and her brother often received blows from their loaded father or angry, stoned mother. Raven suffered the most and started to run away from home. She would be gone days at a time. She found escape in her building at her friend's upstairs apartment. She'd also find safety when her Aunt Bertha picked her and her brother up on the weekends, holidays, or just for different visits during the week.

Raven learned of her aunt six years ago. She marveled at Aunt Bertha's gorgeousness. All of Bertha's nieces did. After all, her hair was always laid, soft baby hairs and edges naturally on fleek. She wore a light coat of Mac powder and shimmer to highlight her pecan-brown, smooth, bright skin. Fur coats lined her closet—brown, white, black, and tan for whatever mood she felt. She had fragrances, purses, shoes, blouses, all the physical accomplishments, but these were only a fraction of her overall beauty. She was beautiful internally as well.

She kept food on the stove and in the oven; everything was home cooked. Her cakes and plates of pasta were made from scratch. "We don't do box or fast food," she'd tell her nieces. "Now get in here and cut these onions."

Bertha kept Bibles in every other room; she was a woman of faith. That was important to her. Her home was always warm and rich in love. She made the house feel like home.

This love was extended to everyone as she cared for others. With a baby on her hip, she cooked and cleaned. She was the example of what a woman looked like and how a woman handled business.

She was all about her business and didn't take foolery lightly. She'd check someone in a heartbeat and fought against injustices of any kind. She was graceful and witty and taught her nieces about men. They loved her stories about dinners on yachts, partying with the politicians, dating golfers, and being a wife, but demanding respect and letting them know how a woman should carry herself. "You could never be bought, honey, he doesn't make enough," she regularly told her nieces.

She demonstrated the value of independence but the smarts and necessity of ego stroking, supporting family, and submission. She taught them what it means to know what you bring to the table and that the importance of eating alone as necessary at times.

She was a seamstress too and could make the most alluring custom outfits, hats, and coats at the drop of a dime. She made curtains, gloves, and everything.

Bubbly, spunky, but very inviting, that was Bertha Matthews. At red lights, she'd shoot a glance at the car next to her, and smile at her nieces before taking off, racing the car beside her.

She celebrated family and life. That was most important to her. She refused to allow anyone to be hungry, abandoned, or mistreated. She was the glue, common denominator, nucleus, mother, aunt, sister, matriarch, and friend. She was everything to her family and especially to her children, nieces, and nephews.

Bertha knew the dire need for Raven and Man Man's well-being. She brought them food, clothing, and toys and assisted with homework. She'd swing by Sunday afternoons to take Raven and Man Man home with her to bathe, brush their teeth, and get ready for the week. She most certainly ensured that they had a hot meal before dropping them back off. Aunt Bertha provided a sense of normalcy for them. Ironically, she had done the same for Danielle and her siblings decades prior.

Like Raven, Danielle had endured much of the same. She witnessed physical and drug abuse. She remembered the same punches Carlos inflicted on her mother, the lines of snorted cocaine, living in filth, cold, and hunger. Those dark childhood memories were Danielle's motivation behind her drive and ambition.

The happier memories were a direct reflection of Aunt Bertha's influence. These moments produced the close bond between Danielle and her aunt. She credited a lot of her success to her Aunt Bertha's support.

Raven felt the same about their aunt in her own way. At times, she wished she could fly away like a blackbird and start a new life. She often loathed what life had offered her and her own existence.

Chapter Four

The Call

~~~~~~~~~~~~~~~~~~~~~~~~~~~~~~~~~~~~~~~

West Midtown, Atlanta

Cracking open a bottle of her favorite Cabernet, Danielle stubbed her big toe against the bottom of the dishwasher.

"Shit, my polish is chipped," she blurted out while jumping in agony.

Tonight was a special night for her as she successfully booked her first television appearance after closing out a crowdfunding campaign, raising more than nine thousand dollars in seven weeks toward her book release. She decided to get dolled up, head to dinner, and celebrate. She started the pregame wine sipping at home while listening to her favorite artist, Sade.

Successful, beautiful, fun, and a sports lover, she'd been single for the last three years. With the move to Atlanta, her schedule and workaholic tendencies didn't help her meet people either.

"I'll date when this book is finished," she often told herself.

It was the same song she sang each year but with a different tune. But this time, she meant it. Danielle had planned to be intentional about dating and to be visible in the coming year.

The oldest on both sides of her family, she didn't have children either. It became tiring at family functions to evade the marriage/baby questions from older relatives. Deep down, it bothered her now and then. She longed for someone to love but stayed submerged in work or new goals. They became her defense mechanism and a way to ignore her dully aching heart.

She found comfort in setting new goals and being creative. Furthermore, it was hard dating in Atlanta with all of the superficiality, gays, pretentiousness, high women-to-men ratios, and reality-star mentalities. She was so over it but did enjoy real conversation when she found it. Danielle had always been more of the sapio-sexual type. Her thing was to be intrigued by witty banter, arts, and mental stimulation. She enjoyed aesthetic pleasure too and loved to see a handsome, fit man.

"Girl, I chipped my freaking polish. I need another outfit. *Errr*, I really wanted to wear these shoes," she huffed at her friend as they locked eyes on FaceTime.

"Dee, calm down, you can wear the shoes. Put a dab of polish on the chip," her friend explained. This was another one of her best friends from undergrad. She knew hundreds of people and had a lot of friends but kept a close circle of best friends. They all called her Dee, but her family called her Danielle.

"Okay, girl, I have to get dressed. I'll let you know if I pull some hot handsome guys later," Danielle chuckled before hanging up and tossing her cell across the purple and grey comforter covering her bed. Slipping her body into a fitted olive midi dress while taking a sip of wine, she heard her cell vibrating again.

"What's up, cuz? You good? Wait! Say what? Like how sick is she? Larry, seriously give it to me straight," Danielle demanded as she listened to the tension in her cousin's voice.

They finally had a moment to chat, but Larry's optimism and denial didn't fully convey the magnitude of his mom's health issues. Now confined to hospital beds, she was failing badly. After several radiation treatments, the doctors couldn't do any more. What began years ago as a persistent cough developed into an uncontrolled growth of abnormal cells in her lungs. Consequently, tumors formed, spreading cancer throughout her whole body. She began to frequently throw up blood and developed massive headaches. Tumors grew on her brain, which swelled as well.

Danielle had no idea but decided to trust her cousin's assurance of "Moms is pulling through, and they're removing all cancer soon." She knew her cousin didn't like entertaining conversations of any kind like that. Even with his health bouts, he kept things simple. Similar to his mom, he didn't want anyone worrying about him. Danielle knew she needed to get up there soon to see her aunt for herself.

They had a special bond. In many ways, Aunt Bertha demonstrated what a woman looked like and how one carried herself—not Danielle's mom, but her aunt.

Danielle was second to the oldest of four by her mother and second to the oldest of six by Carlos. Her parents had three children together—two girls and a boy. Carlos exited their lives when she was five.

Nearly twelve years older than Danielle's mom, he controlled and abused the woman who was just a teen when they met. Two years later they conceived Danielle. As a result, Danielle grew up under seriously adverse circumstances and in poverty. She watched young as her mother and Carlos fought, consumed drugs, and dwelled in chaos.

Aunt Bertha often provided safety, refuge, and even shelter to Danielle, her mom, and siblings. Acting as a mother figure even to Danielle's mom, she wanted better for them. Bertha encouraged and supported Danielle's mother in relocating from Chicago, leaving Carlos for a fresh start. It was Bertha's love that kept Danielle and her siblings alive.

"Yeah, she'll shake it real soon. Otherwise, how's the family, cuz?" Danielle insisted in efforts to lighten the mood.

"They're good. We're all good, just waiting for Moms to recover. I ran into your pops the other day."

"Who, Carlos?" she sighed. "Just say 'Carlos'; he hasn't earned the title of 'pops.' How're his kids? I'm going to try and swing by when I get in town." In her excitement, she wanted to tell him about the television interview, but she didn't think the time was appropriate. "I'll be there next month for a little book business and press. Hopefully, I can see Auntie or the kids then."

"Yeah, that would be good. You big time, cuz. You really doing ya thing. We're all rooting for you here. Yeah, go see the kids when you can. They not doing so well, and Ma haven't been able to stop by there lately."

He didn't mention the fact that it had been nearly a year since she'd been consistent in supporting them. Between Bertha's doctor's visits, her health, caring for her small grandchild and sister, Raven and Man Man were put on the back burner. She wasn't able to keep up like she used to. They were surviving but at risk to be taken by Family Services at any time.

Raven had recently been jumped by five older girls and severely bullied. She didn't want to live anymore. Man Man got into trouble daily and was heading down a dark path. They were growing more and more into products of their environment. They needed intervention fast.

"Hey, cuz, I have to run. I'll see you when I get there next month. I'll keep you posted when I'm planning to arrive. You be strong. I am praying for all of us. We need Auntie to shake this, and she will. Love you."

Masking her true emotions for the sake of Larry, tears now trickled down Danielle's makeup and into her wine glass as sipped slowly, reflecting on the conversation. She felt numb and helpless. Thinking the worst of both her aunt and the kids, she began crying harder and harder. She moaned with the uncertainty of how ill her aunt really was. She thought about what would happen to the family if anything happened to her. Aunt Bertha *was* the family.

Danielle also cried over the hurt of not being able to support her siblings in the way she wanted. She was frustrated and angry at Carlos for his absence in her own life, his selfishness, and how the kids were living now.

Swallowing down more wine, she reflected back on the day she first learned she had more siblings.

"Raven, this is your big sister; her name is Danielle," Aunt Bertha introduced the pair with a smile.

"Hi, pretty girl, how old are you?" she uttered while extending her arms to hug her. Raven ran over to Danielle with a big smile, putting up three fingers.

"She doesn't talk much, but she's three. I keep telling Carlos they need to be in somebody's school," Aunt Bertha said.

"Wait, 'they?' Is there another child? How many other children does he have? How many more siblings do I have?" Danielle demanded.

"Raven has a brother. I think he's ten months or something. They just started coming around. Well, I started going to get them when I learned they were out there. I'm shocked your father is still having babies. You know he had a testicle removed years ago."

"Um, okay, spare me. Where are they living, and where is the mom?"

"They live over on 63rd and Lowe in Inglewood. She on that stuff too, had all her other babies taken away."

"Wait, more siblings?"

40

"No child, they weren't by Carlos. He's been messing with her for years, but these are his last. I been working to make sure they don't get taken away. I need my family to stay together. This is why I'm telling you about them now."

Carefully inspecting the little brown toddler in her arms, Danielle thought, *Wow, this girl looks just like me.*

Raven then hugged her big sister very tightly before kissing her on the cheek. At the time, Danielle had just graduated from college and moved back to Chicago to begin her career. She was only twenty-four.

She hadn't seen Carlos in years. The last time they talked was her sophomore year in college. At the time, he claimed he wanted to get clean and to have a relationship with her. Initially, Danielle thought his wish was genuine. She longed for this but later learned he was manipulating his sister, Bertha, to appease her. Carlos often did this when he wanted something.

Before that conversation, Danielle had likely talked to him last in high school. They didn't have a relationship despite Bertha's efforts to foster one. She thought about her upbringing. Danielle suffered from absent father and abandonment issues growing up. The lack of her father's presence made it difficult to trust men although she sought validation from them. Danielle was no longer bitter, but growing up, she was. As an adult, the news of more siblings made her sad.

Again she examined the little girl in her arms. The affection that Raven displayed for Danielle was heart-warming. She held onto Danielle as if they had known each other for years. There was a connection, and Danielle took a mental note to check on her periodically. But fresh out of college, she wasn't in a position to do much of anything at the time.

Vrrrrm. Her vibrating cell snapped her out of her daydream. It was her sister, Pee Wee, calling to congratulate her on the crowdfunding and television interview. She looked at the phone before texting, "I'll call you later." She wanted to get her emotions in check after hearing such news. She also didn't want to alarm any family members until she saw Bertha herself.

Danielle knew how discreet her aunt was about things like that. She also knew Larry only told her because it had to have bothered him badly. He was very stoic but trusted his cousin. He respected her. She decided not to mention anything.

Getting up to wash off her makeup, Danielle decided to stay in for the evening and finished the bottle of wine.

CHAPTER FIVE

MAN MAN

~~~~~~

Chicago, Illinois

Severely ashy and cracked eczema skin covered Man Man's dark body. Wearing his favorite faded brown T-shirt, he ran barefoot down the halls of the fifteenth floor. When he wasn't following his big sister around, he darted in and out of friends' apartments. Man Man was very impulsive and hyper at best. He was well known in the building and had friends on every floor. He was the funny kid that got into fights. He suppressed his internalized anger and then perpetuated violence. However, at just eight years old, he didn't have the means to identify this or express himself. Carlos wasn't the best role model, but Man Man adored and looked up to his father. He took his every word as gold.

And what spoke loudest were the nonverbal lessons of mooching and the characteristics of what a man shouldn't be.

After all, Carlos showed him how to "pimp slap" a woman, hustle, and how to con people. He showed Man Man how to hand-wash his underwear while delicately placing them in the oven to dry without burning them.

Man Man enjoyed the attention that came with telling funny jokes and being full of personality. He wasn't very confident and was often cynical. And he didn't think much of himself, so when he fought or made people laugh, that fulfilled him. Rarely the initiator, he always found himself laying haymakers into someone's face.

Sometimes, it was his smart mouth that got him involved. The older boys in the neighborhood picked on him frequently. But they soon realized he had no filter, chill, or in-between. If someone hit him or his sister, if he was frustrated, or if he felt threatened, he went for the jugular, every time. His parents told him to anyway.

Furthermore, in the jungle of his neighborhood, it was always about self-preservation. Underneath the emotional debris, Man Man was genuinely vibrant, brilliant in many ways, and very precocious. He thought on a high level for an eight-year-old. His exposure and having older parents put him ahead of his time. Still, Man Man longed to be protected, validated, and loved.

Running down the halls, knocking on random doors, and dashing off before they answered, he was a prankster as well. He practically knew everyone in their twenty-two-story building. The lady in 1503 was his favorite. She made him sandwiches some days after school. Older and frail, she was on drugs and in an abusive relationship. She had a one-year-old who Man Man and Raven took turns babysitting.

"Everyone in our building does that stuff," Man Man said knowledgably to the school counselor. She asked him a series of questions to learn more about his living conditions. They started to meet weekly in this dusty wooden office in the back of the school where the floors creaked when you walked on them.

"Does what stuff?"

"You know, that white stuff," Man Man stated, looking at the floor.

"What did you have good to eat last night, Jabarry?" Ms. Jackson, the counselor, changed the subject. Jabarry was Man Man's government name. No one called him that except for teachers at school. Everyone else called him Man Man. Ms. Jackson was new to the school and took her job seriously. At least, this is what Man Man thought about her. She was never late to their scheduled appointments and always followed up at the next visit with what they previously talked about.

However, Man Man was smart enough not to give her too much information. It was a typical practice not to have people "all in they business" like his mother would say—not even if they were trying to help. He didn't trust too many people at all but played the role well come counseling sessions. When he had bruises, he hid them.

He knew if he was honest, Ms. Jackson would've tried to get his parents in trouble.

"Don't let those white people get me in trouble. You want your father taken away and locked up again, hon, Man Man?" The thought of Carlos's voice uttering this had him visibly shaken.

"I had something well balanced and delicious. Now can I go?" he demanded.

The times when Raven ran away, Man Man defended himself at home. He lay on top of his sheetless bottom bunk in the dark, rubbing his dirty feet together. He enjoyed watching flies land on and off the broken, dim street light outside his window or watching planes flying in the night sky.

Man Man loved everything related to transportation and wanted to be a pilot or truck driver. He had a fascination with automobiles, planes, and trains. "I'm going to make lots of money when I get big," he often said. He believed that money was the key to happiness and success.

Although time alone gave him an opportunity to think, he dearly missed his sister. He loved and admired Raven so much. They were indeed all each other had. They played together, fought, and did normal mischievous kid things. Most importantly, they loved each other profoundly and stuck together. They feared being taken away or separated and did everything in their power to stay together.

On warm days, they would scrounge up enough change for two popsicles before walking to the corner store after school. Playing in the busted fire hydrants was a favorite pastime. Together they hid from their parents, slept on Aunt Bertha's couch, colored, and stayed up talking together each night. Although he got on her nerves, Raven loved her little brother just as much as he loved her.

Chapter Six

Terminal C

〜〜〜〜〜〜〜〜〜〜〜〜〜〜

**Hartsfield Jackson International
Atlanta**

"So I found the perfect gallery to have the party," Danielle blushed with excitement.

"Girl, where?" her sister, Pee Wee, asked.

"It's going to be in the West Loop at this dope art gallery with an exposed brick wall, multiple levels, and a stylish freight elevator that I'm going to turn into a bar. I want to have spoken word poetry, signature cocktails, large painting-size book excerpts, and a DJ."

"You are forever doing the most, but continue," her sister interrupted.

"Just tell my brother-in-law he's keeping the kids, and girl, get yo freakum dress ready! This party is going to be lit! Hey, I have to run, my plane is boarding. Love you." Danielle powered off her phone before boarding the 757 plane en route to the BWI airport.

She was heading to DC to do a couple of radio interviews and to catch up with some old friends. Dragging her little KTSU handbag from undergrad, she thought, *Sheez, I need to get new luggage with all this traveling coming up.* She grabbed the first window seat she could find and gazed into the horizon, thinking about how successful her book would be.

Danielle was very passionate about mentorship and working with youth, specifically inner-city teens. She wanted to be who she needed growing up and to make a difference in underserved communities. Reflecting on her days working for Chicago public schools and with DC public schools youth, she remembered how fulfilling her work was. She had aspirations to travel across the country to motivate and speak with teens.

Heading to DC was exciting for a couple of other reasons. Not only did she have book promoting to do, but she also hoped to see a male companion. Just in case they connected, Danielle packed a fitted black dress and a pair of stilettos.

His name was William. She was a couple of years older than him. They had met years ago in Houston. He was six feet tall with brown skin and very handsome. He had the most beautiful pearly white teeth and curly eyelashes. He was an ex-football player with a fantastic physique. He was a little rough around the edges but college educated and respectful. He was in law enforcement and from Southeast DC. William was single, spontaneous, and charming.

A date night, conversation, or some type of get together was just what she needed to relax during the stress of planning her book release party.

Her girlfriend, Devita from undergrad, picked her up from the airport. They stopped at a trendy bar on H Street for cocktails and conversation before heading in that evening.

"Wow, Dee, you're literally months away from publishing this book, girl. *Eeeeeeeek!*" Her prissy girlfriend squealed. Flipping her exaggerated bang, dressed in everything pink and green, she hugged Danielle tightly. "You've been talking about this book since TSU. I remember everything. Omg̲g̲g̲g̲g̲. How are you feeling? What's the plan after your release?"

"Why are you so extra?" Danielle chuckled, mocking her friend. "Omg̲g̲g̲g̲g̲, I need to have a shot of that clear crap you're drinking. Seriously though, I'm nervous about my next move. I mean, what am I going to do with myself, and is this thing really going to take off like I envision?"

"I think so! Girl, anybody in their right mind would support you. Shit, people going viral for twerk videos, but when someone talking real change and impacting culture, everyone is silent. This is why your message is so needed."

"Tell me about it. No girl, the worst is not being bookable due to how many people follow you on social media. What happen to real content?"

Vrrrrmmm. Dee's phone vibrated once before she looked down and saw that it was William.

"Hi, beautiful, you in my city yet?" he texted.

"Girl, William just hit me. What do I say? I don't want to sound thirsty. He asked was I here yet."

"Tell that ninja to come drop it in yo drawlz," Her friend chuckled. "Seriously, though, let me see your phone," Devita said while snatching it from Dee's hand.

"Mr. Officer, I didn't know this was your city, but I'm here (smiley face emoji). What time are you picking me up?"

Devita quickly hit send before Danielle yelled, "Wait, let me see!"

"Oops, let us get you home and dressed, girl. We'll have the check." Devita stood up, signaling the waitress.

"So you ever been to King's memorial?" William asked while opening the passenger door of his matte-black, two-door Porsche coupe. The license plate read, "Ill Will."

Staring at his broad shoulders and back muscles, Danielle had to compose herself before responding. *Damn, he smells good*, she thought. "No, I've never been." She blushed before he closed her door.

She reached over to open his, and they both laughed when he got in. "Girl, you must've been watching *A Bronx Tale*," he smiled.

They had an amazing time, visiting the King Memorial, Lincoln Memorial, and the Washington Monument in the night sky. Luckily, she brought flats because they did a lot of walking. They talked about the book, his family, the good old days, and she opened up about her Aunt Bertha.

"I don't know what would happen to the family if something happened to her. She is my father's side. I mean, I feel so terrible for my cousin, Larry; he shouldn't have to deal with this stress on his heart. I feel terrible for all her sons but especially him."

William was very empathetic, engaging, and supportive. He grabbed her tightly, smothering her in his big arms while assuring her that everyone would be fine.

Her mood lightened up as he picked her up, displaying his strength. He lifted her a couple of times before letting her down. They laughed in between gazing into each other's eyes.

Danielle had to be at the studio early the next morning, so the night ended with a kiss. William didn't plan to let her off the hook quickly. "Wait, I want a kiss this time." He smiled. She kissed him for the first time.

Danielle had always been curious about the texture of his lips but kept things flirty but cordial between the two of them. She liked and enjoyed him but knew they were on two different pages. Not only were they miles away from each other, but his life-style would have been tough to deal with. William was a workaholic just as much as Danielle was. She also thought his job was too dangerous and unsettling for her. Furthermore, William wasn't truly ready to settle down. She refused to set herself up for failure by entertaining a serious relationship with him. Instead, she planned to enjoy the night and the moment as much as she could.

She savored all the beautiful feelings and positive vibes he exuded. Their kiss was magical. His lips were indeed soft and all she hoped they'd be.

Danielle slept soundly that evening before getting up before dawn the next morning. She was up drinking coffee and trying to settle her nerves as she waited for her Uber to arrive.

Minutes later, she made it to the studio and took a deep breath before walking in.

"You're listening to *Point Blank Period* in the Radio One Studios 1450 WOL, and we have a lovely guest in the studio today. The talented, beautiful, and very intelligent author of *Dreams Bigger Than Texas*. Ms. Danielle, tell the people a little about yourself."

Chapter Seven

Syrup Sandwiches

~~~~~~~~~~~~~~~~~~~~~~~~

63rd and Lowe
Chicago, Illinois

"Raaaaaven, can you help me get this syrup down? I'm trying to make a sandwich," Man Man yelled from the small, dirty kitchen. They were left home for hours, starving and fending for themselves. That's what they hated most when school was out. Summer breaks meant idleness and hunger. They didn't have cool summers like the kids on the North Side, other communities, or kids in private school. They never took family trips or summer vacations. They were confined to their block, neighborhood, and comfort zone. They lacked exposure, resources, guidance, and the opportunity to be kids. Raven had larger issues on her mind and so did her brother, Man Man.

At that moment, Man Man was all about quieting his rumbling stomach. He stood there, figuring out something to eat, and he knew a syrup sandwich would do.

The kitchen floor was stained, with a stench of sour milk fuming from the sink. Raven just woke up from a second nap. Exiting their bedroom, she stomped on a group of baby roaches piled together, feeding on a sticky substance on the hallway floor. Their dim, eight-hundred-square-foot apartment reeked of urine near the bathroom and was infested with cockroaches.

Before they had a sofa, they had a bedbug infestation due to the mattresses that took up space in their living room. Carlos used to allow transient friends stay the night, crashing on the mattresses for a small fee.

"Man Man, we ain't got no bread. What you trying to make?"

"Sandwich," Man Man yelled.

"I'll go find some. Stay in here and only open the door for me when I come back, okay?" Raven instructed.

She pulled back the heavy steel door as she mumbled, "We don't never have nothing." Her first stop was to the lady in 1503, but the elevator took entirely too long, so she took the stairs a flight up.

"My mama ain't home, and we hungry. Y'all have a few slices of bread till my mama get her link (electronic food stamp deposit)?"

"I'm sorry, Raven, we ain't got none either." She knocked on door after door, struggling to find two slices of bread for her brother.

Raven sighed as she thought about what she had to do next. She left the building in her father's oversized, ragged house shoes to walk to the store on the corner. She crossed alleys, picking her way over a busted glass, used condoms, and other debris lying on the ground. The weather had started to change as summer progressed. Chicago summers were very unpredictable. You never knew what you'd get. Raven had on an oversized T-shirt and a pair of shorts. She planned to only take a couple of slices from the store instead of risking getting caught with an entire loaf.

Entering the store unnoticed, she walked directly to the back before grabbing a loaf of bread. Setting the loaf on a shelf, she quickly opened it and observed her surroundings. Luckily, the store had quite a bit of traffic flowing through, the perfect cover for Raven. She managed to stuff five slices in the band of her shorts. She wasn't concerned about squishing it as she was determined to feed her brother and herself.

Leaving the bread open on the back shelf, she hurried out and proceeded to run home unnoticed. By the time she reached the building, she had grabbed the squished bread from her waist and protected it with one hand, heading for the elevator. Entering the small elevator, she saw the boy from 1602. He and a group of his friends, ages fourteen to sixteen, were notorious for harassing little girls in the building. Raven locked eyes with him before quickly putting her head down. Surprisingly, he didn't say a word to her. Maybe it was the prayer she muttered under her breath, asking God just to let her make it home.

The elevator stopped on Raven's floor, and she hustled off toward home. She knocked hard three times before Man Man asked, "Raven, is that you?" He let her in, smiling and asking what took so long.

"Boy, hush, I got us bread, didn't I? Even got an extra slice."

They enjoyed their syrup sandwiches and laughed together. Man Man practically drowned his sandwich in syrup. He loved syrup, condiments, and sauces on everything.

They were home alone another six hours before they needed to figure out plans for dinner.

Raven was innovative when it came to creating a strategy for them to eat. She always had something up her sleeve or an idea for them to explore. Quite honestly, she exercised her power as the oldest. Man Man became her puppet most of the time and did what she said. They had been through a lot together, but nothing would prepare them for the news of their aunt's illness.

The pair jumped at hard pounding at the door. Man Man grabbed his baseball bat and, standing in front of the door, demanded, "Who is it?" He was too short to reach the peephole, so he wanted to be prepared.

"*Shhh*, Man Man, don't say nothing. Let them think no one's home, so they can go away."

"It's Larry. I'm trying to speak with Carlos," the voice answered.

Raven grabbed a crate from the living room to stand on, checking the peephole before verifying it was her cousin. "Uncle Larry," she smiled as she opened the door. Because of the large age difference between them, Raven and Man Man called their cousin "uncle."

A bit disheveled, Larry entered the small apartment. Raven instantly noticed something was off. Her cousin wasn't the smiling and vibrant guy he typically was. "Is Carlos here?" he asked, hugging Man Man.

"Nah, they went to make some money. They been gone all day," sighed Man Man.

"Hmm, yeah, I'm good, Rae," Larry smiled as he kissed Raven on her forehead. "So, y'all been home alone all day? Y'all hungry?"

"Yep, we want McDonald's," blurted Man Man.

"That's no problem, lil man; we'll run and grab y'all some. Tell yo pops he needs to go see his sister ASAP when he gets back. Better yet, tell him to just call me."

"Is everything okay with Auntie Bertha?" Raven inquired.

"Man Man, throw on some shoes so that you can make this run with me," Larry demanded, changing the subject of Raven's question.

"Ain't nobody been messing with y'all, right? Everything else good? Y'all pass to the next grade?" Peppering them with more questions, Larry fought the uneasiness he felt at seeing them. He wished he could do more for them, but the stress of his own children, family, and now the added burden of his dying mother consumed him.

They assured him that they were okay as instructed by their parents when someone asked about them and that they both passed to the next grade. They loved their Uncle Larry and enjoyed being around his children who were younger but fun. Man Man especially looked up to and adored Larry. He enjoyed listening to the firefighter stories and wanted to drive a fire truck someday. The kids held a mutual place in Larry's heart. He loved them more than they knew.

Dropping Man Man back off, Larry handed him forty dollars.

"Give Raven twenty. Don't let ya parents know you have it. Hold on to it in case y'all get hungry tomorrow. And don't let nobody cheat you either. You sure you got the food and drinks?"

Larry knew any money the kids had, their parents took.

"I got it," replied Man Man. He fist-bumped his cousin before grabbing the bag and vanishing into the building.

CHAPTER EIGHT

LIGHTS, CAMERA, ACTION!

WGN Studios
Chicago, Illinois

"**I** want everyone to know their past doesn't have to dictate their future."

"Well, there you have it. Danielle, thank you so much for joining us and inspiring our youth."

"Clearrrrrr," the director yelled.

Beaming with excitement, Danielle stepped off the set, thanking the staff and asking her mentee, who had accompanied her, how she had done. She completed her first television interview and had about an hour to travel from the North Side to the South Side. Heading to "The Talk of Chicago," 1690 WVON, the trip overall was short but productive.

Before arriving, she realized she wouldn't have time to see her aunt. Moreover, she was terrified at what she'd potentially find. Even so, the uncertainty and her ignorance about Bertha's health gave her a slight peace of mind. She decided to get through to the release date without anything happening. Danielle ignored the potential lingering reality in the back of her mind.

The release was only three months away, and Danielle wanted to be in a positive headspace. She needed to stay focused. She planned to see the kids and her aunt the next trip. In the meantime, she handled business, visiting the release location and meeting up with her public relations rep. The trip home to Chicago was a success.

Every visit back felt more nostalgic but most importantly, surreal. Growing up a bit nomadic, Danielle called a few places home. But Chicago was where her heart was. It was home. Home! She loved the culture, energy, and beauty of the city despite the negative violent press it had consistently received in the media.

Danielle saw hope and gems tucked away in even the roughest communities. Previously working with youth in both the South Side and the West Side, she had her ideas of how to stop violence and poverty in the city.

She preached employment, mentorship, and exposure as keys. "If they don't know what's available out there, how can they know what to aspire to be?" she said in many interviews.

Although she lived in a very different middle-class Chicago from her youth, the issues they faced weren't foreign to her. She grew up just like them but turned out differently. If anything, their differences were what bred passion about change within her. She wanted to teach people that they too could rewrite their stories.

Her trip ended with several glasses of whiskey and laughter with her favorite cousin Larry, her friends, and brother, Lil Carl. Every time she came back home, she hosted everyone for get togethers. This time was no different except now she was just months away from becoming a published author.

They laughed, sipped, and chatted the night away. She always had a great time when she connected with Larry. She knew he needed a breather, and she wanted to provide that. They didn't talk much about Bertha that night. Instead, they enjoyed each other's company.

En route to the airport the next morning, Danielle thought of her little siblings. They didn't have a close relationship, but she cared for them. The age gap was significant. Between grad school and working, her schedule became crazy over the years. They didn't get a real chance to bond.

Additionally, Carlos was notorious for spewing hurtful words at her, which contributed to the division. He'd condemn her for doing well or accuse her of thinking that she was better than he was. The times when she stopped by but didn't give him money upset him the most. It wasn't that Danielle couldn't handle the insults. She just preferred to avoid the drama. Raven was seven and Man Man was five years old when she moved to Atlanta.

She reflected on coming over to their building from time to time. Danielle brought food, toys, and read to them. During some visits, she sat for hours until their parents came back.

The kids were often left by themselves. This bothered Danielle, but in the back of her mind, she knew the kids would be okay. She thought about how she and her siblings turned out fine. Deep down, she placed confidence in their Aunt Bertha's presence when she moved to Atlanta. She figured that, as long as Aunt Bertha was near, they'd make it.

In the meantime, she took turns getting the kids as Aunt Bertha did. She came around somewhat consistently in an effort to know them.

And Raven lit up every time she saw her big sister. Making her way to Danielle's lap, Raven plopped down, hugging her tightly. She hardly said a word but always smiled, tightly holding on to Danielle. Her affection spoke much louder than words could.

Man Man brought his cars out of the bedroom, anxious to show off his accumulated toys. He talked the most or asked to play with Danielle's phone. They enjoyed the times their big sister came over, and she enjoyed seeing them.

They were often in her thoughts even while she was in Atlanta. She hoped her book would be a success, putting her in a position to better assist them someday.

Chapter Nine

F*ck Cancer

~~~~~~

Rush Medical Center
Chicago, Illinois

Mumbling incoherently, Carlos uttered, "Bertha Matthews," for the third time in frustration to the receptionist.

Put off by his appearance and body language, the receptionist firmly asked, "How can I help you?" before surveying the two children he had with him.

"I'm here to see my sister, where is she? What floor is Bertha Matthews on?"

"Five," the receptionist said.

Attaching the visitor pass securely to Man Man's T-shirt, he gripped Raven's hand, and they headed for the elevator.

Exiting the fifth floor, Carlos's heart raced with anxiety and concern. This was the first time in a long time Carlos felt anything beyond his daily euphoria.

They entered the room to see a frail Bertha Matthews who had just returned from physical therapy.

"Auntie Berthaaaa!" Raven ran toward her aunt before the nurse stopped her.

"Gently! Hug her gently. She's tired, lovely," the nurse insisted.

"What happened to your hair?" Man Man asked, staring at his aunt in curiosity.

"Man Man, have a seat," Carlos instructed.

Locking eyes for some time before looking away, the reality of his sister's condition punched Carlos in the gut. Inside, he ached with guilt. He wasn't doing well at all, seeing her like that. Carlos had been distant and arrogant, displaying entitlement toward her for the last couple of years. He acted as if she were responsible for his children and cleaning up the messes he made.

But at that very moment, in his sixty-three years of life, he wanted to trade places with her. He wished that he were in the hospital bed, not her. *She's such a good person. She doesn't deserve this*, he thought. He loved his big sister, and although he rarely expressed it, he was grateful for all that she had done for him and their family.

Bertha talked slowly but steadily to them. "I trust God until He says it's time." She felt her brother's sadness and knew deep down he wished he could've been better. They were close growing up, but his choices in life stunted their relationship.

Born in the decade of heroin, later evolving into the war on drugs, Carlos's father and uncles were addicts in the 50s. He and Bertha had different fathers but the same mother. They grew up with different views on life. While Bertha did the home-making and supporting their mother, her brothers ran the streets. Consequently, Carlos was intro-duced to drugs at a very young age. Watching both his father and uncle indulge, he became an addict too.

Smoking and snorting away brilliant potential, Carlos dropped out of school early. This led to a more significant path of self-destruction.

The times he wanted to turn his life around, he didn't. Without an education, trade, or guidance, the fast life was most comfortable. And the feelings of inadequacy, guilt, and failure kept him using. Carlos tried to subdue these feelings with drugs. However, the drugs only blossomed into a perpetual cycle of more erratic behavior and magnified his problems. Bertha knew this, which created a soft spot for him all these years.

Lying there, Bertha had the same look their mother had before she passed, the look of death. Physically, she didn't have much to give. She knew her days were numbered, and so did Carlos. They both felt it.

"How is your mother, and did y'all eat today?" Bertha asked Man Man. Caring and compassionate as always, she was thinking of them despite her health.

She offered them her hospital tray and instructed them to split the gelatin.

Distracted, Raven noticed a small blackbird that landed on the window sill near Bertha's bed before responding.

"Mama's okay," Raven finally uttered.

Bertha became visibly exhausted, resting her eyes and speaking more slowly. Carlos noticed her struggle, which made him more panicky at the thought of that surreal moment.

"What am I going to do with them? Who go keep up with these kids?" Carlos sighed in frustration.

Bertha heard him but proceeded to rest her eyes. She didn't respond.

Man Man and Raven exchanged glances at their father's words. An uncomfortable and awkward silence always followed after hearing him talk like that. His words pierced deep and made them feel unwanted. Still, they loved him unconditionally.

Raven began to sob at the thought of losing her aunt and being unwanted by her father. Her young mind couldn't fathom what would happen to them without Bertha. She missed her aunt's presence that year.

Raven and Man Man had no clue of what was going on. But seeing her frail body stretched out in a hospital bed helped to put things in perspective. It made sense why they hadn't seen her lately. Raven had so many things to tell her aunt. In the last year, things seemed to worsen at home as she thought of her aunt's absence. Carlos became far more physical and impatient with her and Man Man. Bertha wasn't aware of the physical abuse they endured. She knew about the abuse to their mother but not toward the children. On many occasions, she told the kids' mother to leave. But Renesha never did.

Silent, Room 503 stood still as everyone watched Bertha resting her eyes.

Chapter Ten

Hey, Girl, Hey

〜〜〜〜〜〜〜〜〜〜〜〜〜

Radio One Studios
Houston, Texas

"Today we have a sit-down special with a very talented guest in the 93.7 studios. She's here to talk about her newest book, *Dreams Bigger Than Texas*."

Danielle sat tall in front of the poster of her book cover. She had been traveling with it for the last couple of months doing promotions.

Being back in Houston provided vibes of confidence and admiration. Houston was like another home for her ever since her college days.

She had been invited to do a couple of radio interviews and some speaking at her alma mater. Things were rolling and in an excellent flow for her. Each new opportunity gave her the needed push of motivation for an epic launch.

"Hey, girl, hey," Danielle squealed, walking into her favorite happy hour spot off Interstate 610. Dressed in five-inch heels, fitted distressed jeans, and a tank top displaying the title of her book, she sashayed over to hug her girls. Danielle's hair was tightly curled and cut shorter in the back.

She went short a couple of years ago after she turned thirty. Cutting and relaxing her natural hair of seven years was transformational. The short hair complemented her maturing style, but the Houston humidity didn't want to let up. Not only did she fly down for press, but Danielle planned to film a video trailer during that visit as well.

Graduating with a degree in radio/TV/film, a lot of her friends worked in the industry. She was connected with the help she needed to shoot her video.

Danielle met up with former classmates, associates, and a couple of close friends at the happy hour spot. Just like the times she visited Chicago, Houston was a reunion. Only this time, everyone was a bit older, talking about their careers, latest vacations, spouses, and showing off pictures of their children.

Many of her friends were newlyweds and just entering parenthood. They were all accomplished HBCU (historically black colleges and universities) grads and redefining what success looked like culturally. They supported each other and demonstrated strong community at its best.

Jokingly, the singles envied the married friends' lifestyles until they were reminded of the beauty of freedom.

"I wish I had a bae to come home to and argue with," one of the girls lamented.

"Yeah, okay, but marriage is a lot of work, commitment, and sacrifice," said the beautiful, chocolate-complexioned girl with the massive four-carat diamond on her ring finger.

As much as Danielle loved the single life, she would have liked to share moments with someone special. Reaching new pinnacles in every aspect of her professional life, she felt her personal life was like watching paint dry at times. Truthfully, she didn't want to attend her book-release party solo at all.

Laughter and drinks continued to flow until she connected with more friends to film her video.

Confident, charming, and assertive, she stood before the camera, thinking of Aunt Bertha, her family, and that moment in time. The director yelled, "Action," breaking into her thoughts and bringing her back to the present.

Chapter Eleven

Dreaming Bigger

〜〜〜〜〜〜〜〜〜〜〜〜〜〜〜〜

Inglewood
Chicago, Illinois

"You little black bitch, you ain't no daughter of mine. You might as well kill yo self! You knocked over my medicine," the frail, black figure hurled insults at Raven. "Won't you go upstairs to your little friend's house?" Going through drug-induced withdrawals, Renesha was irate at the fact that Raven accidently knocked over the white powder that sat on top of a saucer, resting on a wooden board that sat on a little crate.

"Ma, she said I can live up there anyway. It's not like you want me here," Raven fired back at her mother before being shoved to the ground and hitting her head on the cold, hard floor. Getting up quickly, Raven ran out the door to escape her mother's fury.

Over-the-top squealing echoed in the hall as she stormed out. Chasing from behind, her mother began swinging at Raven but didn't connect the punch. Raven was quicker than her mother. A neighbor who planned to notify Family Services opened her door to observe Raven running down the hall to the stairwell after hearing the commotion. "I'm never coming back," Raven yelled.

She entered the stairwell with a little plastic knife. Slowly placing it to her wrists, Raven cut herself over and over, intentionally aggravating the still-unhealed cuts on her arm. Sobbing uncontrollably, she finally cried herself out and fell asleep in the desolate, dingy stairwell.

Downtown Chicago

"The elevators on the left will take you straight to the fifteenth floor, and the bellman will be up shortly with your bags. Please enjoy your stay."

Grabbing her purse and room key, she surveyed the lobby. Danielle had always admired the culture and spirit of Chicago. Treating herself to a five-star hotel, Danielle looked around. The hall was mainly decked out in Cubs paraphernalia with some Bears memorabilia as well. The Chicago Cubs were in game three of the World Series vs. the Cleveland Indians, and the Bears were playing Monday night football at Soldier Field. Halloween was the same weekend, so the city was packed, energetic, and excited. To make things sweeter, Chicago was unseasonably warm for that time of year. At 72 degrees, Danielle couldn't have asked for a more perfect weekend to have her party.

"The view is amazing, and I'm glad this weather is perfect. I thought Chicago would be freezing this time of year," her girlfriend said, drinking alcoholic concoctions from a white foam cup. Danielle had driven up with a friend from Houston. They met in Atlanta before taking the eleven-hour drive to Chicago.

Danielle arrived a week early for press and last-minute preparation. Her friends and family were coming shortly from DC, Ohio, Houston, Nashville, and Atlanta. With over two hundred RSVPs, she was looking forward to a sold-out release.

After carefully doing her makeup, she dressed in her first press look before heading to a radio interview. Although excited, nerves held her stomach hostage for the majority of that day. Her thoughts were with her family. She planned to see her siblings and aunt later that evening.

Chapter Twelve

Everything Is Fine

Inglewood, Chicago

"Raven, I'm going to ask you a couple of questions. I need you to be honest with me. We've talked to your brother already."

Ms. Jackson, the school counselor, had her arms folded across her chest. Raven partially faced her, refusing to make eye contact. She was exhausted and still shaken up by a shooting at her building that took place last week.

A guard got into an altercation that led to a couple of men open-firing at him in daylight. At the time, Raven and a friend were playing only feet away. She remembered the pop of distinct gunshots before throwing herself on the ground as the window shattered. The guard's body hit the concrete. He bled out from his chest onto the street.

Raven watched his lifeless body and imagined herself being shot as well. She wondered if anyone would care if she were shot. Raven often asked if anyone cared about her. She frequently had thoughts like this. Raven didn't believe her mother or father cared for her. At times, she felt her brother hated her too.

In her quiet time, she asked God why no one loved her. Since the shooting, it had been days since she'd slept at home. Raven was scared and becoming increasingly depleted by life and all the fighting between her parents lately. She and her brother were at odds as well. They made severe threats toward each other. Raven was even convinced that Man Man would push her out of the window. In reality, they were just frustrated and took it out on each other. The kids were hungry, tired, angry, and feeling hopeless.

The weight of Bertha's absence became more prevalent than ever. School had recently started back up, and they faced the year without new clothes, shoes, or needed supplies. This made them a target for more bullying. The kids in their building and at school teased them for being dirty and for having minimal belongings. Bertha usually took care of new and clean clothing and shoes for them.

Carlos used more to cope with the illness and absence of his sister. He was desperate, unpredictable, and often erratic. Consequently, Man Man and Raven's mother was too. She took out her anger from Carlos on the kids. They both became more physical and verbally abusive toward the kids. The four of them were living in complete chaos. Just weeks prior, they had been without water and electricity for days.

That caused one of the older residents in the building to notify the school. She told the school about the fighting and drama that had been going on at the children's home. This started the beginning of interrogation of the kids and investigation by the school's staff. The new counselor was committed to doing her job and was genuinely passionate about youth.

But the kids knew what to say to avoid getting in trouble. At times, Raven wanted to confess it all. But she knew there would be consequences. Raven wondered how bad things would be if she and her brother lived with someone else. On the other hand, Raven still loved her parents.

As soon as the thought of leaving popped into her head, Raven feared that her parents would go to jail or that she'd be separated from Man Man. Worse yet, she'd heard horror stories about all those foster care and group homes and had nightmares about them.

For that reason, she answered the counselor's questions with very misleading and sarcastic responses before asking to leave for the day.

Raven and Man Man met near the rear exit as they always did before walking home. She told her brother she'd catch him later and to listen to whatever their mommy said. "Keep them happy, Man Man. If they're taking medicine, stay out the way."

Carlos referred to drugs as "medicine," but Man Man and Raven knew what "medicine" really was.

Man Man headed home, and Raven stayed on the elevator before going to her friend's. She often stayed at her friend's apartment for days at a time.

Man Man came in, tossing his folder on the couch, and began taking off his shoes. The door was unlocked when he arrived, and no one was home. He knew that usually meant his mother was down the hall, and Carlos was out hustling money. Man Man sat on the couch, looking out the window at the train passing by his home. A knock came at the door, and Man Man hopped up with his bat before answering, "Who is it?"

"It's Danielle. Man Man, you can let me in."

Opening the door with a bashful smile, he said, "Hey, Danielle," as she reached out to hug her half brother. She focused intently on the little second grader before her who looked just like she left him. His hair was very nappy, uncombed, and not picked. Man Man's eczema-covered arms were dry and ashy. He was barefoot, topless, and wearing a pair of stained, flooded uniform pants. They embraced for a second before she inquired about everyone else.

Standing up, Danielle kept her purse zipped and in hand each visit. She didn't want roaches climbing in it. She didn't even like to sit on their couch. The times she did, she sat on the edge with her legs crossed. Their home reminded Danielle so much of her childhood and the dilapidated surroundings she and her siblings lived in with Carlos.

Moments later, Man Man's mother walked in.

"Man Man, Raven, y'all here?"

"Hi, Renesha," Danielle said cautiously.

Embarrassed and placing her hands over her face, Renesha looked at Man Man before inquiring why he "hadn't cleaned up."

"I think he just got in from school, and we were talking," Danielle said.

Danielle proceeded to defuse the situation by asking Renesha how she had been. Antsy and appearing to be going through some withdrawals, the frail figure went on a rant of how bad things were.

She was a master manipulator at best. This rubbed Danielle the wrong way nearly every visit. If she wasn't asking for money or providing a sob story, she put the kids up to asking for "school-related money." Danielle caught on some time ago after realizing they never truly spent the money she'd give for the kids. In fact, it made Danielle angry and resentful about her interactions with Renesha and Carlos.

Prior to moving to Atlanta, picking the kids up was a gamble for Danielle because when it was time to drop them back off, no one was visible. Therefore, Danielle limited her visits to short ones over to their building. She never felt comfortable leaving them alone. The whole ordeal was frustrating and tiring.

Danielle briefly listened to Renesha before asking where Raven was. Renesha couldn't truly answer the question but suggested, "Maybe she's at friends."

Carlos walked in shortly after. Stopping in his tracks, he laid eyes on Danielle for a brief second before mumbling something under his breath.

"What was that?" Danielle asked.

"The fuck are you doing here if you're not planning to take these kids with you? Take them and don't bring them back," Carlos demanded.

"Excuse me?" Danielle countered in complete shock. She had not seen her father in years, and that was the first thing that came out of his mouth. She was sick of excusing his behavior and of being the bigger person.

Danielle felt her face flushing with anger, but she kept it cool in front of Man Man. "Hey, Man Man, how is school?" she asked. This was to divert attention from herself. Inside, she choked with fury and hurt feelings. Danielle tried to be mindful of the occasion that brought her home in the first place. She still hadn't faced her aunt but went through a myriad of emotions standing in the presence of her father and half brother.

"Come here, Man Man," Danielle extended her arms to hug him before telling him she'd stop back by to see him again before she left town.

"Renesha and Carlos, tell Raven I stopped by," Danielle said before opening the heavy metal door to let herself out.

Quickly walking to the elevator, she was stopped by Renesha. "Danielle, I don't know what got into him, but we're doing bad. You got a couple of dollars to spare so that I can get a few squares?" she inquired. Danielle looked the frail, black woman in the face while holding back tears.

"No," she answered simply before getting on the elevator.

Chapter Thirteen

Deep Breaths

Rush Medical Center
Chicago, Illinois

Taking deep breaths as she put her rental car in park, Danielle held a quick conversation with herself.

Aunt Bertha, I just want to thank you from the bottom of my heart for all that you do and have done.

No, girl, where is your faith? She's not as bad as you think. She'll be home cooking by Thanksgiving.

Whatever you do, don't look shocked or sad. Be uplifting. Aunt Bertha could use high spirits and positive energy. Exiting her car, she took another deep breath before walking in.

"Hi, what floor is Bertha Matthews on?" Danielle asked the receptionist.

"Go to five and hang a right as you exit the elevator," the woman said, handing her a visitor's pass and ink pen.

The elevator ride felt like an eternity. Danielle found herself struggling to swallow just as the doors opened. The clicking of her heels hitting the cold hospital floor echoed across the hall. Everything appeared to be in slow motion. Finally arriving at Room 503, she spotted a very frail and lifeless brown-skinned woman stretched out in a hospital bed. She was wearing a jean hat to keep her bald scalp warm and thick layers of socks covered her delicate ankles and feet. Bertha was unrecognizable and looked drastically different from the woman Danielle knew and loved.

A cousin who was visiting from Colorado greeted her. "Hey, Danielle, girl, get in here."

Hesitating, Danielle hugged her relative and responded. "When you get in town? I didn't know you were here."

"Well, hi, Danielle," Aunt Bertha's strong voice announced. "How is your mother?" Utterly shocked by how healthy her aunt sounded, Danielle was comforted by the greeting.

Although Danielle hoped for a private moment with Aunt Bertha, she enjoyed the little time with visiting family. She wanted privacy to tell Bertha about the book signing and what she had been up to the last year. Instead, she silently watched her with sadness and surrealism. Aunt Bertha's voice was always comforting, assertive, and active. Although her voice didn't match her current appearance, Bertha's voice gave Danielle a sense of peace to keep going. Danielle wanted to believe everything would be okay.

For the time being, they laughed, chatted, and admired each other until it was time to depart. Telling her aunt she loved her, Danielle kissed her on the forehead before leaving.

Over the next couple of days, Danielle remained very busy with interview after interview until the big day of the release.

Celebrating hard the night before, she enjoyed her friends and family. The day of, she especially enjoyed intimate quality time with her little sister, Pee Wee. They were very close and only eleven months apart. Pee Wee was a confidant, wife, and a fantastic mother. Even though Danielle was the oldest, she admired her little sister. As they talked, she broke the news about their Aunt Bertha.

"She looks pretty bad. She doesn't even look the same, Pee Wee. I'm trusting God for a miracle turnaround in health," Danielle said with tears in her eyes. Pee Wee consoled her, ensuring her their aunt would be back in the kitchen cooking by Thanksgiving. Pee Wee wasn't as close to Bertha as Danielle was but loved her the same. Pee Wee was usually more emotional than her big sister Danielle but took the news fairly well.

They continued bonding by getting their makeup done before picking up last-minute items for the book release. Danielle's closest friends arrived early to support her with setup and preparations. As the event began, people started entering and browsing the art and book excerpts placed throughout the gallery. The decor was quaint, sophisticated, and sexy, just like Danielle imagined.

She had signature cocktails, giveaways, and a DJ who played all the melodic tunes. The makeshift bar created on the service elevator worked perfectly. One of her friends served as the bartender, tossing up the best cocktails of the evening. She had raffles, prizes, desserts, sultry entertainment, and great vibes.

Dressed in a high-collared, deep U-cut, fitted black dress, Danielle rocked an exposed zipper in the back. She wore a classy pair of pinstriped black, white, and yellow pumps and gold jewelry. She looked regal, elegant, and every bit the published author. Surveying the room, Danielle blushed as she greeted the crowd that came out to support her. Soon the gallery was packed out with young professionals, former students, family, coworkers, and even high school friends. The crowd was beautiful, engaged, and vibrant.

A local artist performed between the MC who got the crowd ready for Danielle's big speech. She was nervous with excitement but calmed down after a bit of reassurance from her cousin Larry.

Slowly walking to center stage, Danielle grabbed the mic. Her exotic hand jewelry and beautifully manicured nails caught everyone's attention. She began to speak.

"Good evening. My name is Danielle Shelton, and I am the author of *Dreams Bigger Than Texas*. First and foremost, I want to thank everyone for coming out and supporting this vision, my baby, my testimony. Many of you tuned into this process about five months ago, some five years ago, and some of you, tonight. The last year has explicitly been a wonderfully brutal, overwhelming yet productive and growing space for me.

"I locked down this project, finishing up in November of 2016. I thought to myself, *How long are you going to procrastinate and let fear hold your story hostage?*

"I started writing in March 2007, just two months shy of graduating with honors from Texas Southern University. After dropping off my application to graduate, I sat there, thinking to myself, *Wow, little old me, the crack baby, the insecure little girl who never seemed to fit in. The one with the challenging past. The one who statistics said would be dead, a ward of the state, in jail, a teen mom, a dropout, or on drugs myself, was graduating again and not just from high school but from college, a four-year university with honors.*

"Now this might not sound like a big deal to you upper-echelon, astute, privileged, elite, silver-spoon, aristocratic, and very well-to-do educated professionals, but this was a big deal for my family and me. You see, my mother's consistent words were, 'You bet not bring no babies in this house and be sure to get your GED.' "

Danielle went on speaking gracefully on her theme for the night of "Dreaming Bigger" as she looked into the eyes of those in the crowd. She concluded her speech with the value of mentorship, inspiring others, and letting people know their past doesn't have to dictate their future.

All eyes were fixed on Danielle. Many were tearing up, admiring her with pride, and genuinely excited to experience the moment. Love and positive vibes filled the room. She managed to finish the entire speech without shedding a tear. The adrenaline kept her pumped. She thought of her aunt's absence but smiled.

Working the room, taking photos, signing books, and hugging loved ones—the release was more than she ever imagined. The night ended at one of her fave bars on the West Side with uncles, family, and friends talking mess, listening to music, and watching the final moments of the Cubs game.

Later that evening, she arrived at her hotel in total disbelief at how well the night had gone. At that very moment, it hit her: she accomplished a nine-year goal. Danielle slipped off her dress and showered before pulling back the linens to crawl into bed. She sobbed silently with gratefulness and joy.

CHAPTER FOURTEEN

TWO MONTHS LATER

~~~~~~~~~~~~~~~~~~~~~~~~~~~~~~~~~~~~~

12/24/16
Atlanta, Georgia

"**H**ey, cuz, they saying Moms any day now," the solemn voice on the other end of the line uttered.

"Whaaat!? Larry last said that the cancer was almost gone, and she was recovering well. What you mean, 'any day?' " Danielle demanded.

"It's Stage IV, Dee; she's been worse off than y'all knew. The doctors can't do anything else for her. She kept it from Larry and everyone as long as she could. At this point, we need to start getting stuff in order. Larry isn't doing well now that he knows the entire truth. You need to talk to him. His wife and I are worried about him."

Danielle hung up the phone after speaking to one of Larry's older brothers. Logging onto her laptop, she purchased a ticket and headed to Midway airport the following day.

Larry was her everything, and she'd do anything for him without hesitating. She valued the closeness he and his mother shared. She also knew how delicate the situation was due to his own health issues. Larry had been recently released from the hospital himself since learning of his mother's illness. Trying not to think the worst, Danielle refrained from asking further questions to keep her peace. But she knew her cousins needed her, and at the drop of a hat, she was heading to Chicago.

Packing a small backpack, her phone vibrated once more. Her brother, Lil Carl, was calling to share more upsetting news.

"Hey, sis, Carlos went rogue, and we think he tried to get rid of Raven."

"What? Get rid of Raven? What are you talking about? What does that mean?"

"It's something with Raven. We can't find her anywhere. They said he tried to sell her to this lady in the building. I called the police already, and they telling me I need to call Family Services. Aaaaaaaah! I'm going to stick around the building until I find her."

"Okay, bro, I'm flying in tomorrow to help Larry. Aunt Bertha is any day now, and he needs me."

"What? Any day?" her brother snapped.

"I have to run. Call them directly or stop by when you can!"

Danielle hung up in a frenzy, rummaging around her apartment, distressed, panicky, and uncertain of what was happening. With Carlos's behavior lately, anything could have happened to Raven. Danielle never experienced a family death or any close loss, for that matter. Therefore, "any day now" felt like a theory. It hurt hearing that but still didn't seem real.

The flight to Chicago was suffocating. Her stomach remained in knots from the commute to the airport until they landed. She picked up a rental car before driving to her aunt's home as Bertha was now in hospice care at home.

Aunt Bertha's home previously felt lively yet quaint and cozy. This time, it felt cold, eerie, and broken. She was greeted by her baby cousin, Bertha's four-year-old grandson.

"Granny is lying down; she has a toothache and don't feel good," the toddler said. Surveying the quiet home, she peeked in her other aunt's room (her autistic aunt that Bertha cared for). She greeted her with hugs and kisses before heading to Bertha's room.

Danielle's heart sank to her stomach as she turned the knob to enter. There she was, propped up on several pillows. The room was dark and smelled like her aunt's perfume. In the background, the television blasted *Alfred Hitchcock* followed by *Perry Mason*. These were Bertha's favorite black-and-white shows. Danielle walked over to admire her once-vibrant aunt.

She was even thinner than before. Her body looked like skin stretched over bones. Incoherent and weak, she groaned in pain, motioning to be rotated. Bertha's oldest son was by her bedside. Turning her face away, Danielle couldn't watch without crying. He lifted his mom before turning her body to the other side.

"Cuz, she needs rotating every so often. Her body is too stiff to be on one side for long amounts of time," he said. "She also likes to be sat up now and then as well. Her cup and straws are to the left. We keep a bowl and tissue by the bed in case she needs to spit and wipe her mouth."

Only hearing every other word, Danielle was drawn to a little blackbird peering through the blinds as it chirped on the window sill. She thought back to one of her fondest memories of her aunt.

"Danielle, grab those lemons," Aunt Bertha smiled. "The trick to real iced tea is to let it sit in the sunlight for hours. You have to make it brew. We'll squeeze some lemon in it after it brews a bit. So tell me, how is everything down in Nashville and starting freshman year of high school?"

Danielle and her family had moved to Nashville, Tennessee, a few years prior. Aunt Bertha had convinced Danielle's mom to leave Carlos, Chicago, and the drugs years before. She wanted her to start a new life for the kids. Danielle distinctly remembered all the moving and how much her life changed for the good as a result in Nashville. She moved around quite a bit as a child.

"School is fine, Auntie; high school is just tougher, and I still can't cook. Pee Wee always in the kitchen with Mama. She loves that stuff." Danielle sighed.

Bertha chucked before telling Danielle, "Child, you'd get better. You keep being responsible. Your family needs you."

"Cuz, grab her bowl, she needs to spit," her cousin snapped her out of her daydream. Danielle watched as Aunt Bertha groaned until she spit and was positioned satisfactorily.

Exiting the room, she asked her cousin how long she had been like that. He said that it had been almost a month now. The cancer came back aggressively and spread throughout her body. He updated her on preliminary plans for Bertha's possessions and responsibilities. But they quickly needed a solid plan of action. Bertha cared for a couple of people and handled all the inner-family workings. Her shoes were much too massive for any one person to fill.

Although Bertha's sons were handling the majority of things, Danielle figured someone needed to step up to delegate and rally the family. Communication was critical, and therefore, Danielle assumed the position by calling a family meeting. Not only did they need to discuss a plan for Bertha's transition, but they also needed a plan of action for her half siblings.

Carlos had allegedly tried to sell Raven for money to buy drugs. One of the ladies in the building claimed that Raven belonged to her and that she already made payments and had papers. Although Carlos denied the allegations, the lady was adamant about not giving Raven back because she had paid for Raven. Danielle's oldest brother, Lil Carl, made this discovery while going to pick up the kids over Christmas break.

After a confrontation with this lady that he didn't know, he and Man Man waited around for Raven after calling the police. They eventually spotted Raven in the building and grabbed her too. Lil Carl fled the building with his half siblings. Dressed in just the clothing on their backs, they didn't take a thing with them.

Lil Carl didn't have a plan of action as he took them. He only wanted them safe. Realistically, he couldn't care for them but vowed to keep them until he figured out a plan. Danielle was livid and disgusted by the entire situation. The stress of her aunt was enough, and now the added tragedy of her father's drama was overwhelming. She was so angry that she wanted to go over to their building and fight both parents. But to stay focused, Danielle kept her aunt's love for family in mind.

That evening, she and Larry met, along with other cousins and relatives to discuss who would take over caring for the individuals that Bertha cared for, funeral services, and more.

Everyone looked at each other solemnly. "Well, first up are Carlos's kids. We don't know everything, but we do know Ma can't take them this time. And whoever that crazy-ass woman in the building is, she can kick rocks. For now, they with Lil Carl," Larry declared.

Lil Carl interjected, "I have them with me, but we need to think long term. I had to call Family Services to come and investigate in the next few days. They're sure to take them away and even separate them. You know that system is terrible and doesn't give a shit about kids. I'll keep them with me as long as I can."

Typically very vocal, Danielle sat quietly thinking of what to say as all eyes turned in her direction. Smacked right in the face with tension and discomfort, a family member spoke up, "They're your brother and sister too."

Danielle responded, "I don't have children, and I live in Atlanta without family, help, or support there. I just released my book, and I begin touring next month. I'll need to quit my job. Working crazy hours wouldn't work with two kids. I can't afford this! I can't!" she huffed.

Swallowing hard, she felt the eyes remaining on her until another relative spoke up, "I'll see what I can do, but it would have to be temporary." The room stood still as guilt, turmoil, and hurt settled in the middle of Danielle's chest.

She then burned with anger at the thought of her father, a man she hardly knew, who was absent in her own life and soon to be missing in her half siblings' lives.

Lil Carl and Danielle considered temporary foster care until they figured out a plan. Everyone knew the kids would've gone with Bertha and couldn't go back to Carlos. So much was going on at once. The tension in the room escalated to arguing and fighting. The rest of the meeting didn't go as smoothly as Danielle hoped. The family was pretty overwhelmed.

Just a room away, Bertha groaned in pain while radiating much strength at the same time. As people disbursed, Danielle made her way back to Bertha's bedside. She cried tear after tear, soaking Bertha's T-shirt.

Danielle visualized Raven and Man Man's little smiles and heard their voices in her head. From the moment they met, Raven admired and fell in love with her older sister. Ironically enough, the last seven years of Danielle's life had been dedicated to mentorship and youth advocacy. The kids needed her. The idea made perfect sense, but Danielle couldn't see it.

The inflection in Bertha's groaning patterns slowly began to change. Although incoherent, she felt her niece's sadness and the tears hitting her shirt. "*Ehh*," she moaned. It was as if she was saying, "Everything will be okay."

Excusing herself from Bertha's room, Danielle chatted with Larry to finalize funeral arrangements. Larry's jovial demeanor was off. His spirit seemed heavy. Danielle felt helpless that she couldn't do more for her cousin. She also wanted to give him space to process. So she headed for bed.

Stretched out on Bertha's favorite recliner, she couldn't sleep. She couldn't stop thinking about her brother and sister. Danielle texted Pee Wee, asking what she thought she should do. Pee Wee assured her that she would support whatever choice she made but asked her not to be impulsive. "Dee, you can't be guilted or allow your emotions to guide you," she texted.

Wrestling with the thought of potentially taking them, she ruled out taking both. "I can't do Man Man," she decided. "It's too much baggage; he's too wild. I can't raise a man. I can't afford this and would need a new job." She continued lying there for hours before barging back into Bertha's room. Antsy and throwing an emotional tantrum, she cried even harder at her aunt's bedside. She cried at the anguish of watching her aunt waste away and at the responsibility she possibly would assume.

After much sobbing, Bertha miraculously opened her eyes and spoke.

"Umm, honey, what are you crying for? Trust God, Danielle. I was diagnosed with cancer two years ago. I'm still here today until I go. Stop crying. How you upset about something that has to happen? Stop worrying and trust that it will all work itself out because it will. You're a smart girl. You know what to do."

After Bertha spoke, she closed her eyes and went back to an incoherent state. Stunned by her aunt's voice and alertness, Danielle was spooked. She stopped crying, said a prayer, and kissed her aunt on the cheek before packing up her stuff. It was nearly 5:00 a.m., and she needed to head to the airport. She knew that would be the last time she spoke to her aunt alive.

The flight back to Atlanta was long and tiring. Sipping a Jack Daniels neat, Danielle began to doze off. She dreamed of three blackbirds flying in a formation over a crowd of people. One was up front, leading the other two.

The lead bird was the strongest one with the most beautiful black wings. Just before waking up, Danielle heard the words, "Don't separate them."

She popped up her head, looking around to see where the voice came from, but no one else was there.

The coming days back in Atlanta were excruciating for Danielle. Bertha and the kids consumed 90 percent of her thoughts. She struggled to eat, sleep, and focus. Danielle was angry with her father and even mad at God. She couldn't understand why her aunt had to die and her father, a career drug addict, still got to live free of responsibilities.

The Super Bowl was rapidly approaching, and she needed to get her head in the game. Danielle planned to kick off her book tour in Houston during the 2017 Super Bowl. It was a no-brainer as the Atlanta Falcons were playing in Houston that year. Utilizing her connections, she booked interviews with a couple of the major stations in Houston. Danielle planned to be strategic and capitalize on the Atlanta traffic in Houston. Intentionality was crucial moving forward.

"Get your head in the game, Dee. You've got this. This is your year. It will be epic, and you've got to be present for it. Do what you can do. Once you're in a better position financially, you can help the kids. They are safe for now, and this book is the priority!" She coached herself with speeches and positive affirmations.

Doing a great job of masking her emotions, she proceeded in public like a powerhouse.

Danielle hardly spoke in detail about her siblings' circumstances. It was a sore spot for her. She struggled with shame and frustration when it came to that. The embarrassment wasn't about the children but about her father's perpetual behavior. The mere thought of Carlos attempting to sell Raven made her furious. She had so many questions about what happened. And the one person who protected Raven and Man Man the most lay helpless and dying.

Danielle carried insurmountable anger. It wasn't healthy, and it started to show on her face. She recognized this and prayed, fasted, and prayed again despite her anger with God. She asked for signs regarding how to help the kids.

Aiming to avoid emotional decision-making, she decided to revisit the idea of taking them in a couple of months. *Give yourself at least six months to think about this*, she told herself.

Her biggest fear was losing freedom, lack of support, and the responsibility that came with children. She was most concerned with the "how." Danielle didn't know how she would afford to raise two children solo while promoting a book and working full time.

The thought was overwhelming and terrifying in itself. In the meantime, she and Lil Carl decided that the kids would go to foster care for a couple of months as they developed a long-term plan. Christmas break was ending, and class was back in session. The kids couldn't stay with Carl much longer. They needed to be in school.

Less than a week after returning to Atlanta, Danielle headed back to Chicago to drop off her siblings with Family Services. Sadly, not one person was available to take them. Carl arranged for them to be picked up as he went to work. But the thought of that made Danielle cringe.

"So you're just going to let some strangers come and take them," she demanded. "They need a proper transition; they are children! I'll do it; I'm booking my flight now."

She flew back to Chicago to transition them personally.

Chapter Fifteen

They Can't Take Us

Chicago, Illinois

"Man Man, you heard what they were saying last night? They trying to get rid of us."

"Who, Raven?"

"Someone called the people on Mommy and Daddy," Raven said with tears in her eyes.

"Raven, what does that mean? They coming to take us away?"

"Yes, Man Man, but I will figure something out. I won't let them take or separate us. We will be together. I hope so because I overheard Carl talking to Danielle."

"I think she coming up here. Hopefully, she can help us. We can't let them take us away."

Raven was dressed in a white T-shirt and pajama pants with her hair standing on top of her head. She hadn't bothered getting dressed as they weren't going to school anyway. Lil Carl had to work and couldn't get them across town to school daily. He couldn't miss any days and needed to keep his job.

"They was also saying Aunt Bertha about to die too, Man Man. If Aunt Bertha die, we're screwed," Raven cried hysterically.

The children were unaware of the magnitude of what was taking place. But after hearing bits and pieces of Carl's conversation, they knew they weren't allowed to go back to their home.

Raven was overcome with discomfort and uncertainty at what was about to happen. They'd had scares before like the time when Carlos went to jail. Or when they had to stay with Bertha for weeks. Or when people came over to investigate. Or, most recently, when the counselor at school started questioning them more. But this time was different, and Raven felt it. The mere thought of losing Bertha was sure to gravely impact their lives.

Raven racked her brain, trying to think of a plan for herself and her brother. She contemplated running away but didn't know where they'd go. Then she decided to beg her brother to stay with him.

Distraught and scared, Raven went in the bathroom and leaned over the bathtub to pray. She began using the words that Aunt Bertha taught her.

"Dear Heavenly Father, who art in heaven, hallowed be thy name. Please, God, let Danielle take us. Let us move with her, Lord, or Carl. Please don't let those foster care people take us away and split my brother and me up.

"Lord, I know I done some bad things to Man Man. I haven't been perfect, but we can't go with those people. God, help us, please." Raven began to cry hysterically, crouched over the bathtub. Man Man heard his sister and entered the bathroom to console her. Despite all their sibling rivalry, he hated to see his sister cry.

The room grew still as Raven's dark-brown skin shivered in Man Man's arms. The sound of dripping faucet water and her brother's voice soothed her worries just a bit. "It's going to be okay, Raven," he said. They sat in silence, just holding each other and taking comfort in each other's presence.

Lil Carl understood the severity of Raven and Man Man's situation as he had a history with the foster care system himself. Lil Carl, who was named after their father, Carlos, went by Carl or Lil Carl. He was Carlos's oldest child and the oldest half brother of Danielle, Man Man, and Raven. They had different mothers.

Carl was taken into foster care at a young age until Aunt Bertha adopted him out of the system and began raising him.

A convicted felon, Carl had a past of his own. He got into some trouble as a teen and worked hard ever since to overcome that label. Lil Carl was a hard-working man who wanted to be a better man and father than his own. He too shared a close bond with Bertha and looked up to her as a mother figure. Carl had his own children and worked strenuous hours. Realistically, he couldn't care for Raven and Man Man. He wasn't able to provide them with what they truly needed. Carl didn't have the time, patience, or ability to commit to such a huge additional responsibility.

As a matter of fact, he couldn't even take a day off to bring them down to Family Services. So he arranged for a pickup. And, Danielle tag teamed to step in.

Arriving at Chicago Midway airport, her heart was beyond heavy. Danielle rehearsed how she planned to deliver the news to the children.

"You know I love you unconditionally, right? Me, Lil Carl, Larry, and Aunt Bertha. We all want the best for you, and right now, that is not being near your parents. You guys deserve to be with someone who will care for you."

No, Dee, that doesn't sound right, she said to herself.

"I'm going to drop you guys off with some people who will look after you for a little while until me and Carl figure out a plan. It is only temporary."

She rehearsed more as her heart rate increased, pulling into Carl's driveway.

She sat in the car a moment to gather her thoughts before calling Carl.

"Hey bro, I just arrived. What is the alarm code?" Danielle asked. "And you haven't talked to the kids at all yet?"

"No, Dee, I didn't wanna mess it up. I haven't said anything. I'm letting you handle it."

"Okay, gotta run. I'll call you later."

Disarming the alarm, Danielle entered the garage before grabbing the spare key to let herself in. She took three deep breaths and slowly made her way into her brother's kitchen. She noticed a half-eaten sandwich, two empty bags of chips, and two cups sitting on the counter. The television blasted with a holiday jingle.

"Wishing you and yours a very happy New Year."

Slowly, Danielle walked up the stairs to hear two little voices talking in the restroom. As she knocked on the door, both Raven and Man Man screamed.

"Stand back, Raven, I got it. Who is it?" Man Man asked.

"It's me, Danielle."

Raven snatched the door open before jumping on Danielle.

"What are you doing here?" Man Man asked, smiling.

Hugging them, she asked how they were doing and if they knew why she was there. Danielle wanted to see how much they knew and where their heads were before opening her mouth. She proceeded to talk to them separately. They both understood they couldn't go back home. They knew they couldn't go with Aunt Bertha and feared not seeing each other again. Both conversations broke Danielle's heart. She wanted to pray with them but needed to move quickly to avoid an emotional meltdown. The three of them held hands and stood in a small circle with their heads bowed and eyes closed. The moment was beyond surreal for them but mostly for Danielle.

Danielle said a quick prayer before loading her rental with large, heavy-duty trash bags of their belongings. She moved in silence. The kids had accumulated quite a few things. Most of the stuff was from family and friends. Some of it was too big, but they needed everything. They had nothing besides the clothes on their backs since the day they left the building.

It was a frosty 25-degree Chicago day. "Hats and gloves, zip up those coats," Danielle said but remained silent for the majority of the drive. The kids kept asking where they were going. Danielle had spoken with a Family Services caseworker half an hour prior who was expecting them. The local office happened to be within walking distance from the kids' building. Man Man lit up as he recognized his neighborhood.

"Danielle, can we stop by the building so that I can see my friends? I wanna grab some of my toys too. Please."

Danielle didn't respond, so Raven called Danielle's name twice and asked, "Where are we going?"

Tears began to well up in Danielle's eyes as she put the car in park. She turned around to face Man Man and Raven before speaking. She talked really slow and steady in an effort to avoid losing it in front of them. Dressed in a gray, long-sleeved shirt, jeans, boots, and a leather jacket, she looked very solemn. The sophisticated, beautiful, once-optimistic Danielle looked bewildered and broken.

Saying precisely what she rehearsed, she told the children that she and everyone loved them and that they didn't do anything wrong. She reassured them that she was working on a plan to take care of them. But they needed to go for now.

Man Man and Raven didn't move, and they stared at one another in silence. In an uncomfortable but firm voice, Danielle said, "You hear me? It's time for you to go."

Man Man reluctantly opened the passenger rear door as Raven refused to get out of the car. Raven and Danielle locked eyes just like the first time they met, years ago. Only this time, Raven knew how to talk and understood what was about to happen.

She had two little braids securely attached to her head with barrettes that complemented her sweater. Danielle had put the braids in Raven's hair just before they arrived. Although a small deed and effort to help Raven look presentable, the hairdo meant so much to Raven. This is because Danielle had fixed them. She adored Danielle.

After locking eyes for a spell, Danielle exited the car and opened Raven's door, slowly grabbing her hand.

"I don't want to go with these strangers, these people!" Raven broke down, crying loudly and uncontrollably. Man Man stared at his sister before beginning to tear up himself.

Danielle could no longer hold in her tears either. The three of them cried as they walked toward the entry door of the Family Services building. Danielle wanted to get the paperwork before returning to the car to grab their bags.

Raven's cries became louder as she refused to walk any further. Nudging and trying to avoid dragging her, Danielle kept walking, pulling Raven's arm. By then, she became hysterical and started to create a scene, crying yet harder as she kept asking to go with Danielle.

"I want to go with you; why can't I go with you?" she repeated.

Ignoring Raven's cries, Danielle managed to get everyone inside of the building. As they entered, Danielle wiped her eyes before being interrupted by a woman she had never seen before.

"Well, well, you must be their sister, Danielle. Hey, Raven!" The lady greeted them.

"I am, and who are you?"

"I been looking after your sister, and she coming with me today. You can keep the boy."

"Keep the boy? What? Raven, who is that?"

Enraged, Danielle quickly realized that this must be the lady from the building—the one who gave Carlos money for Raven. Ignoring the woman, Danielle walked past her and requested to speak with the social worker she had been communicating with.

Pleading her case, Danielle told the social worker, "A strange lady is trying to take my sister." She expressed her concerns about not knowing the lady and wondered if she wanted to indeed help and why she wasn't taking Man Man as well.

"It's dangerous for them to be in that building near their parents." Frustrated and unable to get all her thoughts out, Danielle kept repeating, "This woman can't have Raven. The kids can't be separated. I don't know this woman."

"Ma'am, we're going to ask you to have a seat while we talk with her and the kids individually. She supposedly has a signed document from your father, saying he gives her rights to take Raven," the social worker explained.

"Rights? What? With all due respect, my father is on drugs, and a signed piece of paper is hardly legal or a court-validated document. Furthermore, I'm sure it's something she wrote and enticed my father to sign for money. Is this Child Protective Services? Y'all are supposed to protect the children. I am their sister, and I don't know this woman!" Danielle felt her heart racing faster in frustration and anger as her feelings spiraled out of control.

"Ma'am, the kids aren't allowed in the home, and if your father signed a document, this is something for us to consider."

"And Man Man?" Danielle interjected.

"Yes, Jabarry, Man Man, whichever you prefer, can begin the intake process this afternoon. Now again, you'll need to have a seat so that we can finish interviewing everyone."

Furious, Danielle stormed toward the seating area, motioning for Man Man and Raven. She felt panicky at the thought of losing the children or of them being split up. She couldn't chance it.

She was scheduled to fly home the following day but was scared to leave. Googling custody laws in Illinois and texting every friend she had practicing family law, she started to feel hopeless.

The social workers finally arrived to speak with the kids. Eyeing the lady with the paper from across the room, Danielle called Carl to tell him everything that was happening. The woman approached Danielle.

"Where were you all this time? Raven has been coming up to my home this entire year. Your father signed to give her to me," the woman from the building said.

Still, on the phone with Carl, he heard her in the background and said, "Those are lies. And if he signed anything, it was after you coached him into it for money to get high."

"Carl, I have to go." Danielle hung up before addressing the lady.

"Ma'am, I don't know anything you have going on, but I do know you will not take my little sister. Or split up her and her brother. If you were trying to help so bad, why are you paying my father to sign a paper? That shit isn't legal anyway, and you won't take my sister."

The social workers returned again. "Ma'am, you will need to fill out our guardianship paper and have the parents sign them in our presence before Raven can go with you. But you'll still need to go down to the courts in the next thirty to sixty days to solidify custody."

Afraid of losing her siblings, Danielle quickly exclaimed, "No! You can't let Raven go with this stranger without question. I'll take them!" she blurted out before realizing what happened.

Time seemed to stand still. The room seemed to hold its breath for a few moments. Raven jumped up, seemingly in slow motion, before running over to her sister.

Danielle was stuck and deep in thought. She flashed back to her five-year-old self, boarding a Greyhound bus with her mom and siblings as they left Carlos to start a new life, decades ago. She visualized her Aunt Bertha cooking for her as a kid. Those fond memories soon turned into images of her aunt's lifeless eyes. She thought about what her aunt would've done in this situation. She thought of how Bertha cared for Lil Carl and her siblings.

"Ma'am, Ma'am," the social worker interrupted Danielle's thoughts. "The only way they can leave with you is to have the parents permit you to take them instead. You and the parents will need to sign guardianship papers in our presence. The same applies either way as the children cannot go home."

Swallowing hard, Danielle decided to stand by her decision. Internally, her emotions were having a field day with uncertainty, obligation, and fear.

"Call them!" Man Man said.

"Yeah, let's go to the building and get them," Raven added.

Danielle told the social workers that she would be right back. Grabbing Raven and Man Man by the hand, they headed for the car and arrived at the building in no time. Luckily, both the children's parents were there. Danielle walked in boldly to face them.

"I'll be taking the children with me and raising them. They will not be separated or anywhere near this place. They deserve to have better, a better life and more opportunities than I did. Carlos, you should be ashamed of yourself! Now I would appreciate it if you grab your coats so we can sign this paperwork."

Neither of them hesitated. They shared a silent ride for the short two blocks back to Family Services.

Sitting across from the rough couple, Carlos barely made eye contact with Danielle. He wore a stained T-shirt, dirty denim jeans, and an undersized, stained blue jacket that barely zipped. Renesha's hair stood all over her head. She appeared to be loaded or coming off a high. Even through her euphoria, she seemed equally as ashamed as Carlos. The counselor proceeded to give instructions and explained what was taking place.

"Because neither of you are in the right state to care for Raven and Jabarry, you are signing a temporary guardianship document that gives Danielle custodial rights. She will relocate the children to Atlanta, Georgia, with her and submit this document to her local court. The temporary guardianship becomes permanent unless you petition the local courts in Georgia. But you'll need to undergo several months of counseling and mediation."

The rest of the words blurred. Danielle tuned out, thinking about the approaching Houston trip and a couple of other engagements she had in place for the year. She was laying the groundwork for her nonprofit, organizing a spring book tour, and starting a T-shirt line. She planned to speak at an eighth grade commencement and, most notably, expected to date. Danielle wanted to officially put herself back on the market. She longed for companionship and a husband.

Sitting there, Danielle watched the social worker's mouth move but she didn't hear a single word. Danielle thought to herself, *You've done it now. Kiss your independence goodbye, but it is the right thing to do.*

Glancing at her father once more, she noticed a look of death in his eyes. It was similar to Bertha's lifeless look. But Bertha's dead eyes came from pouring out to others and giving life while Carlos's came from draining life from those around him and even himself.

"Dis only for a little while, Danielle. Ima get myself cleaned up and get my kids back," Renesha blurted out belligerently while snapping Danielle out of deep thought.

Ink from their signatures barely dried before Danielle started putting a plan in place. First, she needed to change flights and contact her job to stay another few days.

Danielle took the time to visit the kids' school and gather birth certificates, Social Security cards, and everything needed to support guardianship and transfer them out of state. Alternatively, Danielle could have relocated back to Chicago. But she didn't want to uproot all that she built in Atlanta.

Furthermore, she figured a change of environment was best for a fresh start. One of her other closest aunts agreed to watch the kids for a month. It was a significant ask, but Danielle was desperate. She needed time to get back to Atlanta to arrange living accommodations, locate elementary schools, find a bigger apartment, look for another job, and do everything else that came with motherhood.

She stepped up to the plate gracefully as with any other challenge she faced. Danielle was resilient, detailed, organized, and refused to lose.

CHAPTER SIXTEEN

HERE GOES NOTHING

~~~~~~~~~~~~~~~~~~~~~~~~~~~~~~

Atlanta, Georgia

Sitting in the tight office space on the eleventh floor of her department's newly promoted director, Danielle felt a tad claustrophobic. She now faced the nerve-racking task of delivering the news to her job. She had been in tunnel vision since leaving Chicago days ago after squaring the kids away.

Calling daily to check on them, they started a countdown to Atlanta. The countdown was pretty exciting for the children although they had never left the city limits or met Danielle's aunt. Therefore, they were living with practically a complete stranger. But Danielle knew they were safe. She stayed a couple of nights with them at her aunt's to help them get acclimated. The children seemed happy about consistent meals, a warm bed, a change of scenery, and shelter.

Danielle's aunt took great care of the children and loved them as her own. She had other relatives help take turns with homework and pick them up from school. It was a genuine community effort. Danielle was grateful for her family and their support of her decision.

But the reality hit her as she arrived back in Atlanta. She had been with the company for a couple of years and established a great rapport with her former boss, who was now the director. He appeared to be very sympathetic and understanding as she spoke.

"Two children. And so sudden. Oh my, Danielle, are you sure?" he asked out of concern.

"Yes, I'll have to make it work. You know me; I'll figure it out." Danielle forced a smile. Inside, she couldn't breathe. She had no clue of where she'd go or what to do next.

"Take as much time as you need. Best wishes and keep us posted if we can help." He smiled reassuringly.

She left the building, heading to Home Depot to grab boxes to begin packing. Surprisingly, Danielle's residence was zoned for one of the top elementary schools in the city, which happened to be nationally ranked. Therefore, she didn't want to leave her community. Furthermore, Danielle didn't have the resources or time to locate a new place to move to anyway. Consequently, she upgraded to a two-bedroom in her complex.

Her friends rallied behind her, purchasing beds, towels, bikes, clothing, and school supplies for the children. They sent money and gift cards, pledging their support. It was an excellent feeling to be loved but also humbling. Danielle had always been the hard-working, prideful, do-it-yourself, super-woman type of person. But the children made her very vulnerable.

She needed help in every area and couldn't pretend she didn't. Because she stepped up to prevent them from being wards of the state, the state wouldn't assist her financially, and she wasn't eligible for much government assistance. It was just her and the kids. So any help was appreciated.

Coming off an incredible year, she would need to defer book plans after Houston. The Houston trip was still on and would be her last promo trip before parenting. She had only been back in Atlanta four days before she got the message that her aunt had passed.

"Hey, cuz, she's gone," Larry texted her.

She sat silently in her car, looking out the window for some time before calling him. They barely spoke, but connected through their tears. The called ended with "I love you," and just like that, Danielle was on another flight to Chicago.

In the days to come, she assisted with funeral arrangements while spending much-needed time with Larry. They went through photos, laughed, cried, and compiled a beautiful obituary. The services were charming, quaint, and intimate. Family, friends, and everyone spoke highly of Bertha's ability to make everyone comfortable. Everyone raved about her cooking and feistiness. She was the matriarch, care-taker, supporter, guardian, and friend.

Dressed in a black high-waist, A-line skirt and a black silk top with a black fur shawl, Danielle wore black leather gloves, black boots, and a black-rimmed hat. Her ruby-red lips set off the attire. She was dressed to the nines although broken internally. Even so, she was feeling as fabulous as her Aunt Bertha would've been externally.

At the service, Danielle took the podium, exhaled, and began to speak about her aunt. Her words were eloquently written and poetic in nature. The leather from her gloves rubbing together produced a faint sound in the microphone. She was nervous as she refused to shed tears while talking. She didn't want to mess up her makeup. Danielle wanted Bertha, Raven, and Man Man to be proud. She wanted them to follow her lead, but realistically, she would only hurt herself in the long run by avoiding grief. She quoted the last words Bertha shared with her weeks before.

The kids were eager and excited to see her. She held them tightly as Raven took her aunt's passing harder than Man Man did. "Raven, sweetie, Aunt Bertha would not want to see you cry. She will always be in your heart, and now we have an angel looking after us. You don't have to worry, sweetie. I will take care of you and your brother. I'll never let anything happen to either of you. I love you, sweetheart."

Glancing into Raven's eyes as she spoke those words, Danielle knew she had done the right thing. She knew that she and the children would be fine. Raven looked beautiful—her hair was nicely braided; she had on pretty tights, a lovely dress, and dress shoes. Danielle's aunt had nicely dressed both Raven and Man Man.

Chapter Seventeen

Blackbirds Fly

~~~~~~~~~~~~~~~~~~~~~~~~~~~~~~~~~~~~

Houston, Texas

"It's always a pleasure to be back in Houston. I was just here a couple of months ago, but I miss and love everything about the city, besides the heat and rain," Danielle chuckled while adjusting her bang.

Recording on Facebook Live, she was in an interview at Majic 102 before heading to the *Yolanda Adams Morning Show*. Grateful for the opportunities, she successfully booked a bit of press that trip. It was essential to Danielle to get her message out. She hoped to reach a few people before going on hiatus.

Danielle stayed with a close friend of fifteen years that trip and needed the bonding time. Soaking up all the parental knowledge and wisdom that she could, she observed her friend and her daughter carefully. Danielle had less than a week to move into a new apartment, set it up for the children, fly to Chicago, and drive them back home before enrolling them in school. Additionally, she needed to start applying for jobs as well.

Fortunately, she was able to secure a temporary consent of absence from her job. The leave provided time to acclimate the children in a routine and a chance to obtain a more accommodating position. The amount of responsibility facing her was exhausting.

All she could think of was life as a parent. Danielle was concerned about the children's social and emotional health. She understood the move would take some adapting and getting used to. After all, they were transferring from a low-performing, under-resourced school on the South Side of Chicago to a more affluent school in Buckhead, Atlanta. They were going from an all-black to a 13 percent black school with vast cultural differences.

Anally organized, Danielle had already planned the children's bedtime and schedule and drafted a contract of house rules. Danielle had folders and daily routines in place in addition to setting weekly meetings with the children's counselors. She had this prepared before they even arrived. As with any new challenge, she analyzed, planned, and faced it head-on.

Super Bowl Houston would be no different despite how she felt internally. En route to Houston, she received a call about her grandfather falling ill. He wasn't expected to live much longer. Admittedly, she wanted to explode but pushed on, using the children as fuel to keep going. Danielle put on well publicly.

"As I always say, you do not need permission to be great, and your past doesn't have to dictate your future. I haven't arrived, but I look nothing like where I've been. My mother's expectations for me were not to bring any babies into her house and to get a GED. She didn't realize she was minimizing my potential down to just that.

"I'm here to encourage people to dream bigger, and you can rewrite your story. Every day is a new chance to reinvent yourself. Your past or even your now doesn't have to dictate your future."

The library of Jake Yates high school was full of students, teachers, and staff. They listened attentively to Danielle's words before taking photos and thanking her for coming. She wrapped up the Houston tour speaking to youth. Exiting the building, Danielle headed toward her car. Her phone rang.

"Hello, Dee, how are you? Are you doing well?" The little voice on the other end of the line asked.

"Hey, Man Man, I am and guess what? We only have three more days until I see you guys and four more days before we drive down to Atlanta. Are you excited? Where is Raven?"

Chicago, Illinois

Raven stood next to her brother, listening to Danielle's voice blasting through the speaker phone.

"We are very excited; I can't wait to start our new life in Atlanta. It's going to be so much fun, meeting new friends, a new city, and school," Raven beamed.

Raven and Man Man were both excited about new possibilities. Although uncertain of what lie ahead, they were ready for the change. Staying with Danielle's family was healthy for them. Consequently, they met a new family who nurtured, loved, and cared for them as their own.

They had no clue of the transformations they were preparing to undergo, but they would benefit immensely: mentally, physically, socially, and most importantly, academically.

Danielle, on the other hand, was in for a tough road that year. Not only would she become an instant mother of two, but she would also go on to lose both her grandparents, start a new job, and lastly, unexpectedly lose her beloved best friend/cousin Larry only five months after his mother passed.

To be continued . . . .

ABOUT THE AUTHOR

After publishing her debut memoir, *Dreams Bigger Than Texas*, author, mentor, and media specialist Rahkal C. D. Shelton went from single career woman to instant mother of two. Losing a close relative to cancer prompted the suspension of her book tour and her introduction to motherhood. Effortlessly, Rahkal is embracing her new role. Her second book, *Blackbird: The Story of a SistaMom*, tells her story.

Rahkal is a proud alumna of Texas Southern University and a graduate of Governors State University where she completed her master's in media communication. Rahkal works in Business Administration for CNN and was previously employed by well-known companies, such as Turner, WGN, Clear Channel Communications, The Smiley Group, and Free Spirit Media. Despite these ambitious accomplishments, Rahkal is proudest of her dedication to community transformation. In 2009, she found her purpose and gift of mentoring and organizing while working for Chicago Public Schools. This discovery led to working with disadvantaged students as well as employees within elite corporate structures, proving by action that she is a helpful guide to both. Her short-term goal is to travel across the country to speak with and motivate youth and young adults. She also plans to start a nonprofit organization that will serve low-income youth, developing them into future professionals.

Made in the USA
Columbia, SC
10 May 2018